THE WASHING MACHINE MANUAL

DIY Plumbing □ Maintenance □ Repair

Graham Dixon

A **FOULIS** Book

First published 1988

Published by:
Haynes Publishing Group
Sparkford, Nr. Yeovil, Somerset
BA22 7JJ, England

Haynes Publications Inc.
861 Lawrence Drive, Newbury Park,
California 91320 USA

**British Library Cataloguing in
Publication Data**

Dixon, Graham
  The washing machine manual.
  1. Washing-machines—Maintenance
  and repair—Amateurs' manuals
  I. Title
  667'.13   TT997
  ISBN 0 85429 633 6 (Jacketed)
  ISBN 0 85429 690 5 (Unjacketed)

**Library of Congress Catalog Card
No.** 87-82792

Editor: Rob Iles
Printed in England by: J.H. Haynes &
Co. Ltd.

Contents

Introduction

The repair and servicing of today's modern domestic appliances may possibly seem a daunting task to perform oneself. This myth consists of several elements:

(a) The mystique created by the manufacturers that their machines are more complicated than they actually are.

(b) The inbuilt fear of electrical wiring that most laymen seem to have (this is not a bad thing as electricity is to be respected at any voltage, and at all times when working on a machine **it must be isolated from the main supply**).

(c) The lack of detailed manuals to suit the person that can overcome 'a' and 'b'.

(d) The fact that if you get past 'a', 'b' and 'c', the parts are – in most instances – difficult to obtain.

At this time, a comprehensive range of 'blister packed' spares are appearing in most good D.I.Y. chain stores, and on public market stalls. As these are manufactured for the general public, they are usually clearly marked with the type of machine and application.

One may be forgiven for thinking that this is a good reason for leaving the repair of your washer to someone who possesses the skills, manuals and parts. This unfortunately generally proves expensive in call-out and labour charges, often only to find that it was a five minute job, with the cost of parts £5.00, and the call-out and labour £25.00. In the customer's mind, £30.00 is little expense for such complicated and unsafe items. Yet their D.I.Y. husband (or wife) will gladly strip down the engine or brakes on their family car, and will take the family out for a drive that afternoon. It is acceptable for car repairs to be carried out by the D.I.Y. enthusiast as the information and parts are readily available. This obviously means that the D.I.Y. car owner saves a labour charge of only to £10 to 15 per hour. Until now, the D.I.Y. enthusiast has been unable to repair any major faults to his automatic washing machine due to the manufacturers and repair companies not wishing to disclose the information. This state of affairs can be remedied by studying the following chapters, coupled with the application of a little common sense. We hope that this manual will be of great assistance in not only reducing your repair costs, but giving the satisfaction which is obtained when a repair is successfully completed.

This manual has been thoughtfully designed to help you understand the function and operation of the internal components of your automatic washing machine.

Flowcharts, diagrams and step-by-step photographic sequences have been used to attain a logical pattern to fault finding. This enables the reader to follow a sequence of events in theory (using the flowcharts), in practise (using the photographic sequences) and in detail (using the diagrams).

This manual will assist you in finding the fault and in giving you the knowledge to repair it. Another important aspect is the regular checking and maintenance of your machine, which is covered in the individual sections, and also a checklist section later in the book.

We hope you will use this manual to assist you in the Do It Yourself repair of your machine. With most repairs you will find it speedier than calling a repair company, and at the same time save the added burden of call-out and labour charges that repair companies must charge to cover overheads and operating costs.

With this in mind, we hope that your faults are few and far between, but remember . . . prevention is better than cure, and regular checks and servicing of your machine can prevent any bigger problems arising in the future.

Acknowledgements

The authors would like to extend their thanks and gratitude to the following people and organisations for their help in the compilation of certain sections.

We would like to thank Oracstar for their help and information that was used in the plumbing section, Persil (Lever Brothers) for allowing us to use sections of their various guides and B & R Electrical Products for their assistance and photographs in the R.C.C.B. section.

We would also like to thank Andrew Morland, who with great patience under exhaustive conditions, produced the excellent examples of photographs that can be seen in this manual.

To those not mentioned by name, but whose help and assistance was freely given and most welcome – thanks. They will know who we mean.

Chapter 1.

Emergency procedures
Safety first

Emergency procedures

With such symptoms as leaking; flooding; unusual noises; blowing fuses, etc., it is best to carry out the following procedure. It is essential that the machine is NOT allowed to continue its programme until the fault has been located and rectified.

Firstly – Do Not Panic

(a) Isolate the machine from the mains supply. That is, turn the machine off, switch off at the wall socket, and remove the plug from the socket.

(b) Turn off the Hot and Cold taps that the fill hoses of the machine connect to. This is done because, even with the power turned off, if a valve is at fault, it may be jammed in the open position. The machine will still fill, as turning the power or the machine off will make no difference to this type of fault.

(c) At this point, the power and water should be disconnected. Even now, if there is still water in the machine, it could still be leaking. Any water that may still be in the machine can be extracted from the machine by syphoning. This is easily done by lifting the outlet hose from its

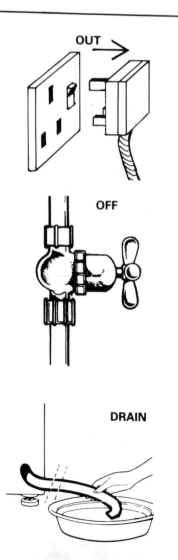

usual position, and lowering it below the level of water in the machine. This will allow the water to drain (unless of course, there is a blockage in the outlet hose!). The easiest method is if the outlet hose will reach to an outside door, where all that is needed is a little movement, and the water should drain. Alternatively, the water can be caught in a bucket using the same technique to drain the water. To stop the water lift the pipe above the height of the machine. Repeat this process until the machine is empty.

(d) Do not open the door to remove the clothes until all of the previous steps have been carried

out, and a few minutes have elapsed to allow the clothes in the machine to cool. In cases where the machine was on a very hot wash, wait about half an hour.

When all of these steps have been carried out, and the clothes have been removed from the drum, it is then possible to calmly sit down and start to work out what the problem may be, and form the plan of attack in a logical and concise manner.

A general safety guide for fitting electrical replacement parts

Switch off! Always withdraw plug and disconnect from mains.

Appliances vary – make sure you have a suitable replacement part.

For screws – use a screwdriver, for nuts – a spanner.

Examine and clean all connections before fitting new parts.

Tighten firmly all screws and nuts (knurled nuts – use pliers).

Your safety depends on these simple rules.

Fuses: Up to 250 watts 1 amp; 750 watts 3 amp, 750 to 3000 watts 13 amp.

Insulation is for your protection. Don't interfere.

Renew worn or damaged appliance flex.

Secure flex clamps and all protective covers.

Test physically and electrically on completion.

Warning: Never leave bare wires outside terminals.

Warning: The wires in a mains lead are coloured in accordance with the following code: GREEN and YELLOW – EARTH, BLUE – NEUTRAL, BROWN – LIVE. As the colours of the wires in the mains lead of an appliance may not correspond with the coloured markings identifying the terminals in the plug, proceed as follows:

The wire which is coloured green and yellow must be connected to the terminal in the plug which is marked with the letter 'E' or by the earth symbol or coloured green or green and yellow.

The wire which is coloured blue must be connected to the terminal which is marked with the letter 'N' or coloured black.

The wire which is coloured brown must be connected to the terminal which is marked with the letter 'L' or coloured red. Use insulated tools.

If in doubt consult a qualified electrician.

Chapter 2.

Tools and equipment
Basic Plumbing
Self plumbing in

Tools and equipment

Modern automatic washing machines do not require very specialised tools. Many of the routine repairs such as blocked pumps, renewal of door seals and hoses can normally be completed with a selection of the following tools.
Crossblade and flatblade screwdrivers,
combination pliers,
simple multimeter,
pliers.

Most people who are D.I.Y. orientated will own one or more of these items already. A useful addition to this selection would be a 'Mole' wrench, a socket and/or box spanner set, soft-face hammer and circlip pliers. These would help with the larger jobs, such as motor removal and bearing removal.

Bearing removal/renewal and the like may also require such things as bearing pullers. As these can be expensive to buy, it is best to hire them from a tool hire specialist for the short period that you require them. Local garages may also be willing to let you hire them for a small fee.

It will not prove difficult to build up a selection of tools capable of tackling the faults that you are likely to find on your machine. Most of the large D.I.Y. stores will stock most of the tools that you require, often at a good saving.

When buying tools check the quality, as a cheap spanner or socket set is only a waste of money if it bends, or snaps in your hand the moment you get it home! Having said that, there are many tools on the market that are of a reasonable quality and are inexpensive – try to buy the best that your budget will allow. Remember – the tools that you buy are a long term investment and should give years of useful service.

As with any investment, it is wise to look after it and tools should be treated the same. Having spent time and money on tools, they should be kept in a clean and serviceable condition. Ensure that they are clean and dry before storage.

Basic plumbing

Although your machine may have been working correctly in its present position for some time, the wrong installation of a machine may cause faults many months later. Because of this time span, the faults are not associated with bad plumbing and can cause the D.I.Y. engineer to look for other faults, which is very time consuming and annoying. Having said this, it is therefore worth examining the existing pipework, and checking the manufacturer's installation details. These details will be found in the manufacturer's booklet that came with the machine. Even if the installation of your machine was left to an *expert*, it is still advisable to read this section, as the chances are that they will not have read the installation details either!

For those of you who cannot find the manufacturer's booklet, below is a brief description of plumbing requirements that apply to nearly all automatic washing machines, and the reasons why they should be adhered to.

If the machine is to be plumbed in "Hot and Cold", then isolation taps must be fitted. This enables the water supply to be cut off between the normal house supply and that of the washer. **Note:** The rubber hoses connected to these taps should be positioned so that they don't get trapped when the machine is pushed back, or rub against any rough surfaces during the machine's operation. Both of these conditions can cause the pipe to wear, due to the slight movement of the machine when in use. Also ensure that no loops have been formed in the hot pipe. In the beginning this will not cause any trouble, but as the pipe gets older and the hot water takes effect, the pipe will soften and a kink will form. This will then cause a restriction or complete stoppage of water to the machine. This can also happen to the cold pipe, although it is very rare due to the increased pressure in the cold system.

The next thing to do, is check that there is adequate water pressure to operate the hot and cold valves. On *Hot and Cold* machines, select a hot only fill. The machine should fill to working level within four minutes. The same should apply when a rinse cycle has been selected. This gives a rough indication that the water pressure is adequate to open and close the valves. This is because the valves are pressure operated, and a 4 p.s.i. minimum is required for their correct operation. The cold pressure is usually governed by the outside mains pressure, but the hot water pressure is governed by the height of the hot

water tank or its header tank. Problems can arise when the tanks are less than eight feet higher than the water valve they are supplying. This is often found in bungalows and some flats. If a slow fill is suspected, check the small filter that can be found inside the hot and cold valves, when the inlet hose is unscrewed. These can be removed and cleaned by simply pulling them out gently with pliers. Care must be taken not to damage the filter or allow any small particles to get past when you remove it. Clean water is normally supplied to the valves, but in many cases old pipework or the limescale deposits from boilers etc., can collect at these points. Kinks and loops can also effect the outlet pipe, and cause several problems to the wash, rinse and spin programmes.

Syphoning is a common fault and can give rise to some unexpected faults, such as:-

Failing to start to wash (always filling).

Excessive filling time.

Programme failing to advance through rinses.

Washing times longer than normal.

The following diagrams show correct and incorrect plumbing techniques, which will cause and cure any syphoning. This also shows that some of the 'major' faults that appear, can be attributed to something as simple as syphoning and can be cured almost immediately.

All of the above faults can be attributed to syphoning, although this may not be the only cause.

Outlet Hose

The outlet hose must fit into a pipe larger than itself, thus giving an 'air brake' to eliminate syphoning. The height of the outlet hose is also important if syphoning is to be avoided. Syphoning can occur when the end of the outlet hose is below the level of water in the machine. This would give rise to the fault of the machine emptying at the same time as filling, and if the machine were to be turned off, would continue to empty the water from the machine, down to its syphon level.

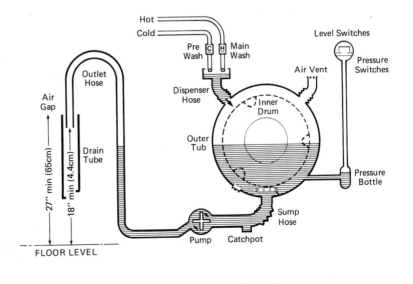

Diagram A – Correct plumbing.

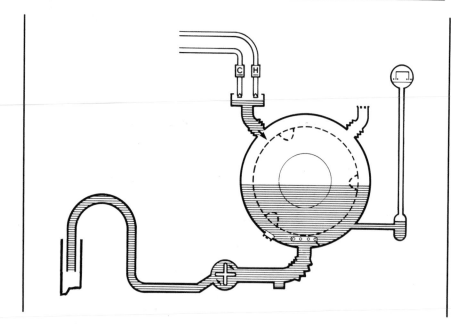

Diagram B – Incorrect plumbing, causing syphoning

Note: Height of outlet hose. Syphoning will take place due to the outlet hose being too low or too far down drain tube.

Self plumbing in

When a machine is to be fitted in close proximity to an existing sink unit, you can take advantage of the new style *'SELFBORE'* taps and outlet systems now available. These simple and effective D.I.Y. fittings will save both time and money.

In most cases, the fitting of these taps can be done with only a screwdriver and no soldering is required. You do not even need to drain or turn off the main water system at all.

At this stage, we feel it is better to give you some visual help rather than pages of text. The following pages show you how easy the fitting of such units can be!

① First, unscrew tap and open clamp.

② Fit clamp around copper pipe in required position. Make sure washer is in position.

③ Engage screw and tighten until clamp is secure. Do not over tighten

④ Insert tap assembly into clamp. Ensure tap is in 'off' position.

⑤ Turn clockwise until pipe is penetrated. Set tap to position required.

⑥ Tighten hexagonal nut towards the pipe. This secures tap in position.

⑦ 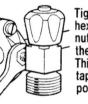 The tap is now ready for use. Connect hose to 3⁄4" BSP thread on tap and turn on.

Plumbing in.

Plumbing out.

Method of fitting

(1) Select the most convenient place in the waste pipe 1¹/₄" (31mm) or 1¹/₂" (38mm) dia.
2. Disconnect components (as shown above). Place saddle halves around waste pipe, removing saddle inserts if pipe is 1¹/₂" dia. Ensure that 'O' ring is seated in recess. Tighten screws by stages to give an even and maximum pressure on waste pipe.
3. Insert cutting tool and screw home (clockwise) until hole is cut in waste pipe. Repeat to ensure a clean entry.
4. Remove cutter and screw in elbow. Use locking nut ⑤ to determine final position of elbow and tighten, or screw non-return valve ③ directly into saddle piece.
5. To complete installation, choose correct size hose coupling to suit drain hose and secure hose with hose clip (not included).
* It is important to remove regularly lint and other deposits from non-return valve. Simply unscrew retaining collar ④

Fitting instructions for washing machine/dishwasher drain kit.

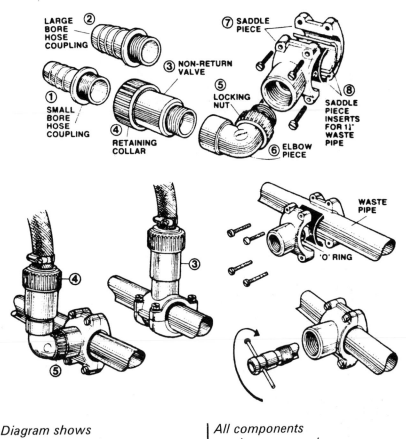

Diagram shows the disconnected components of PK30 Drain Kit.

All components can be unscrewed by turning anti-clockwise.

Discharge into a combined sink and washing machine trap.

This trap allows water from the sink to drain away as normal but has an extra branch for attaching the washing machine hose.

Siroflex anti-syphon unit.

This unit provides an in line air break to prevent syphonage occurring via your appliance drain hose. Full fitting instructions are supplied with every unit.

This information has been kindly supplied by *ORACSTAR*, a leader in the field of Self Plumbing kits, whose wide range of D.I.Y. fittings and accessories can be found in most leading D.I.Y. stores.

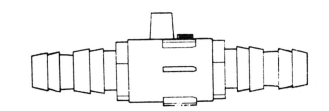

Chapter 3.

Back to basics

Back to basics

Whenever possible the symptoms of the fault should be confirmed by the operation of the machine up to the point of the suspected fault, whereupon the machine should be stopped, disconnected from the mains supply and the relevant flowchart followed. For major leaks, blown fuses, etc., this is *not* practical (more damage may result by repeated operation of the machine). In these cases, the fault is known and further confirmation would be of little benefit. This may in fact, result in further damage to the machine or its surroundings.

Being able to assess and locate a fault may at first seem a difficult thing to do, but if a few simple procedures are carried out prior to starting the work, they will help cut down on the time spent on the machine. Hopping in a random fashion from one part of the machine to another, hoping that you will come across the fault and subsequently repair it, is hardly the best approach to repair work. This is not the way to tackle any job. Without doubt, the best method of fault finding is to be gained from your own experience of the machine, the fault with it and its location and rectification based on all the available information. Always remember a methodical approach to the work in hand, saves time and effort by unnecessary replacements based on guesswork.

However there are a few things that can be done before such testing. These will ascertain if, in fact, it is the machine itself that is at fault or if an external/user fault is the cause. Indeed, a large percentage of repair calls, are in fact, not a fault of the machine at all. Before jumping to conclusions, pause for a moment. You will not only save time and effort, but money as well.

Please remember these points when starting a repair.
(1) Always allow yourself time to complete the task in hand.
(2) **Do not cut corners** at the expense of safety.
(3) Try to ensure adequate working space whenever possible.
(4) Make notes about the position of the part to be removed, the colours and positions of wires, bolts, etc.

If you can acquire this practise, it will help you in all of the repairs that you carry out, not only with your washing machine.

Remember: Good work practises give rise to good repairs
A few simple checks.
(a) Check – That the machine is turned *on* at the electricity socket.
(b) Check – That the fuse in the plug is intact and working. This can be checked by replacing the suspected fuse with one out of a working item of the same rating.
(c) Check – That the taps are in the *on* position.
(d) Check – That the door is closed correctly, that a wash cycle is selected and the knob or switch has been pulled/pushed to the *on* position.
(e) Check – That the machine is not on a 'rinse hold' position or 'short spin' position. On most machines this will cause the machine to stand idle until instructed to do otherwise.

If the fault still remains, the next step is to determine its true nature, and subsequent repair.

Chapter 4.

General care and attention
Regular Inspection points

General care and attention

For many repairs it is best that the machine be laid on its front face or side. Generally it is best to lay the machine on the side opposite the timer. (The timer is located directly behind the main programme knob). This is to avoid the tub and drum assembly coming in contact with the timer.

Always ensure that the outer shell of the machine is protected with a suitable cover when attempting to lay the machine down. The machine should be lowered slowly, to avoid excessive movement of the suspension. When lowering the machine it is a good idea to place a strip of wood under the top edge of the machine, to provide room for the fingers for lifting the machine back into its corrrect position after the repair.

When laying the machine over, care should be taken to protect oneself from injury. Firstly, ensure that the machine is completely disconnected from the main supply, and that the inlet and outlet hoses are removed. Secondly, before attempting to lay the machine over, decide if you you need any help. **Washing machines are very heavy and a little help may prevent a slipped disc.** Thirdly,

before attempting to move the machine, **ensure that the floor is dry.** A wet floor has no grip, especially if any of the water is soapy.

The correct rating of fuse must be used as per the manufacturer's instructions. As a general guide, the applications for the three main ratings of fuse are listed in the general safety guide section.

Plug wiring must be connected according to the following code to ensure safety.

The colours are as follows:
Live – brown.
Neutral – blue.
Earth – green/yellow.

The authors would like to point out at this time, that any references to manufacturers' names or model numbers, etc., that are used throughout this manual are for the reader's information, and *reference purposes only.*

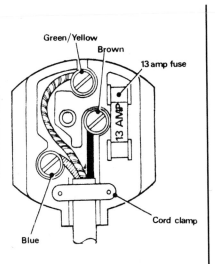

Whilst every precaution has been taken to ensure that all information is factual in every detail, the authors cannot accept any responsibility for any errors or omissions appertaining to this manual, and shall not be responsible for any damage or injury caused whilst using the manual.

Regular inspection points

A regular internal inspection of your washer, may enable you to identify a part that may not be running properly, or find a perished hose before a leak occurs.

It is recommended that the following points be checked regularly.

Inspect	When	Special notes
Pump filter (if fitted)	Weekly	As per manufacturer's manual. Often dependent on usage.
Valve filters (hot and cold)	6 months	If dirty, pull out with pliers and wash out.
Door seal, door glass	6 months	If seal is tacky to the touch, seal may be in need of renewal soon. Rub any sticky fluff off door glass with non-abrasive pad.
All hoses	6 months	As above. Ensure that all corrugations in all hoses are checked thoroughly.
Pump and sump hose catch pot	6 months	Check for any items that may have collected in or at these points. Remove as necessary.
Suspension	6 Months	Check suspension mounts on tub and body of machine. If slide type, see suspension section.
Motor brushes (if fitted)	6 months or yearly	Check for wear and/or sticking in slides. If below half normal length, renew.
Belt tension	6 months or yearly	Check and adjust belt tension if necessary. See last page of the section: Tapered bearing change.
Level machine	Yearly	Check that the machine is standing firmly on the floor, and that it does not rock. Adjust by unscrewing the adjustable feet, or packing under the wheels.
Check plug and connectors	After every repair	After repair, look for poor connections in the plug and socket. Also look for any cracks or other damage. Renew as necessary.
Taps and washers	After every repair	Check taps for free movement, corrosion and/or leaks.

Chapter 6

Determining the fault
Fault finding reference guide

Determining the

Throughout the manual, flowcharts are used to aid the fault finding process. The location of faults will become much easier as you become more conversant with your machine, i.e., through regular servicing of your machine before faults have arisen.

Selecting the correct flowchart for the job will be easier if it is remembered that faults fall into three main categories, Mechanical, Electrical and Chemical.

Mechanical faults

These will normally become apparent by a change in the usual operational noise level of the machine, i.e., a faulty suspension may cause a banging or bumping noise. A broken or slipping belt (incorrect tension) may give rise to excessive spin noise or little or no drum rotation. This may also indicate a drum or motor bearing fault.

Mechanical faults

These fall into two major categories:-

Chapter 5.

Using a flowchart

Using a flowchart

Flowcharts are used throughout the book, and are designed to help you quickly locate the area or areas of trouble, and to show that a step-by-step approach to even the most difficult of faults, is by far the best way to ensure they are found and rectified easily.

The use of flowcharts to those with some experience of home computers will need little explanation. To those of you who will be seeing them for the first time, here is how they work.

How flowcharts work

To the uninitiated, the use of flowcharts may seem a difficult way of fault finding. This is not the case, and will be quite simple if a few small, but important points are remembered. As you will see in the examples, there are only three main types of symbols used. A rectangular box, a diamond and an elipse. With a little practise, you will become aware how invaluable this method can be in all areas of D.I.Y. work. The construction of one's own flowchart before

attempting the job in hand, will be of help when the time comes to reverse the stripdown procedure, i.e., notes can be made next to the relevant boxes on the flowchart, of what was encountered at that point, i.e., number of screws, positions of wires, etc. Small points – but so vital, and so often forgotten with an unplanned approach.

The rectangular box

This is a process, i.e., in the box is an instruction. Carry it out, and rejoin the flowchart where you left it, travelling in the direction indicated by the arrows.

The diamond

This asks a question, i.e., if the answer to the question in the diamond is "yes", then follow the line from the point of the box, i.e., the box asks if a pipe is blocked. The junction to the left is marked "no". and the junction to the right is marked "yes". If the pipe is blocked, follow the line to the right.

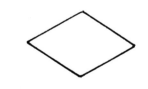

The elipse

This is a terminator. When this box is encountered, you either start a new chart or finish one. The text in the box will indicate the action.

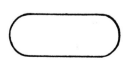

The following example flowchart illustrates the steps involved in carrying out the simple task of opening a closed door, and closing an open door. The arrows indicate the direction to the next step, so as to guide you through the logical sequence.

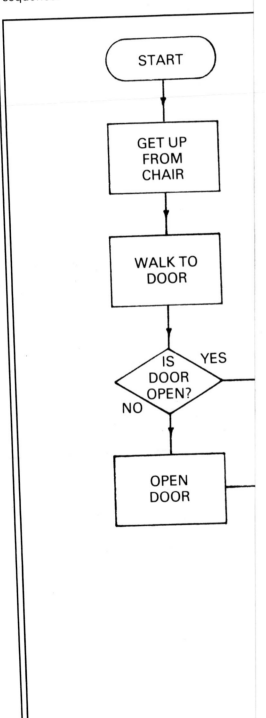

the timer.

Always ensure that the outer shell of the machine is protected with a suitable cover when attempting to lay the machine down. The machine should be lowered slowly, to avoid excessive movement of the suspension. When lowering the machine, it is a good idea to place a strip of wood under the top edge of the machine, to provide room for the fingers when lifting the machine back into its correct position after the repair.

Shown is a simplified flowchart of the operation described on the previous page.

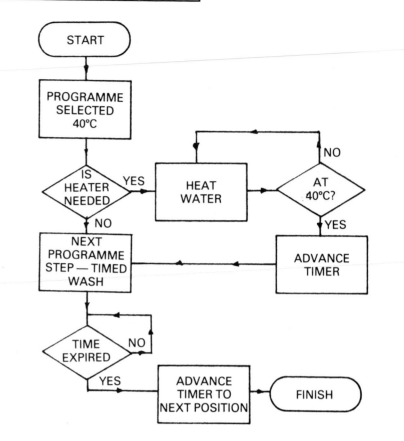

Fault finding reference guide

Machine will not work at all.
Back to basics.
Interlocks.

Machine leaks.
Emergency procedures.
Leaks fault finding.
Pressure systems.
Pumps.
Motor speeds.
Inlet valve fault finding.
Suspension.

Machine will not empty.
Emergency procedures.
Pumps:
Basic plumbing.
Harness faults.

Machine washes but no spin.
Interlocks.
Pumps.
Main motor
Main motor speed control.

Machine will not turn drum.
Check drive belt.
Main motor.
Main motor speed control.
Interlocks.

Machine spins on all positions.
Module control.
Main motor.
Programmer/Timer.

Machine will not fill/take powder.
Back to basics.
Inlet valve fault finding.

Machine does not wash clean.
Check belt tension.
Common causes or poor wash results.
Basic plumbing.
Pump.

Machine is noisy.
Noise faults.
Drum bearings.
Main motor.
Suspension.

Machine won't move through programme.
Thermostats.
Heater.
Inlet valve fault finding.
Programmer/Timer faults.

Machine sticks through programme.
Basic plumbing.
Pump.
Inlet valve fault finding.
Programmer/Timer.

Machine blows fuses.
Emergency procedures.
Low insulation.

The lists below the main fault headings indicate the sequence with which they should be examined.

shown by a small brown rust patch on the top of the valve.

Box 8:

The tub seal and grommets are to be checked now. This means the seal or seals that fit between the separate parts of the main tub assembly. In addition to these seals, small rubber grommets may be found. These will have been fitted to block "machine holes" that are used in the manufacture of the machine. If these come out or leak, they should be replaced or have sealant applied to them. If the large tub seals leak they should also be renewed. This type of repair is described in the section: DRUM BEARING CHANGES.

Box 9:

Any corrosion or flaking of the enamel covering of the outer tub can be treated with a good brand of rust inhibitor, taking care that it does not come into contact with any of the internal rubber hoses, etc., and is used in conjunction with the manufacturer's instructions. Places to note, are where the brackets for the motor and the suspension are welded onto the outer tub. These are stress points where the enamel may crack and flake, and rust will inevitably form. By the time a leak has started at these points, it is too late to save the outer tub, and it must be renewed completely if a lasting repair is to be made. *It is felt that the occurrence of tub renewal on today's modern automatics, is very rare. Therefore, the need for a lengthy section in this book would be unnecessary. Also, the cost of such items and all the relevant seals and parts necessary to complete such a repair would not be cost effective.*

If the machine still leaks after these checks, please refer to the sections: BASIC PLUMBING and MAIN MOTOR SPEED CONTROL.

Exploded v assembly.

1 Door se
2 Clamp
3 Spring
   clamp b
   bolt or
   type).
4 Front tu
   and pos
5 Tub lip
   locate o
6 Dispens
7 Dispens
8 Outer tu
   tub weig
9 Top tub
   Location
10 Carbon
   main bea
11 Front dr
   (ball bea
12 Front be

Chapter 7.

Leaks fau

Noise faults

Leaks

This fault is b
causes the m
inconvenienc
leak/weep ca
parts of the m
floorboards, c
cupboards ov
whilst appeari
normally. Abo
factor of a ma
machine with
be considered.
leak, regardless
must be check
A very small a
may be the cau
is possibly dam
motor. The hos
been inspected
stated in the se
INSPECTION F

With the al
flowchart can b
first it may seen
the leak is comi
would still be w
flowchart throug

Box 1:

The smalles
door boot (door
cause of the big
condition of the
be checked and

Noise faults

Noise can be one of the first signs that something is going wrong with your washing machine. Noise faults are easily ignored, and over a length of time can be accepted as the norm, and because of this it is important that noise faults be examined immediately.

As with other faults, noise faults become easier to locate the more conversant that you become with your machine.

Noises and their most common locations

A loud grating or rumbling noise would indicate a main drum bearing fault. See the sections: BEARING REPLACEMENT.

A loud high pitched noise would indicate a main motor bearing or pump bearing fault. See the section: MAIN MOTOR and PUMPS.

A noise just before and after spin, would indicate wear or water penetration of the suspension mounts. See the section: SUSPENSION.

A squeaking noise mainly during the wash cycle, would indicate a poorly adjusted drive belt. Instructions on how to adjust the drive belt appear on the last page of the section: TYPICAL TAPERED BEARING CHANGE.

Coin damage

Coins and other metal items are easily trapped in the machine, and can cause a great deal of damage. These can become trapped between the inner drum and outer tub, and should be *removed before damage to the drum occurs.*

Coin damage can be identified by small bumps on the inner drum or a rattling noise when spinning. On enamel drums, this may be accompanied by small flakes of enamel in the

Typical coin damage to a drum. This kind of fault can be easily avoided by careful checking of pockets, etc., prior to loading the washer. If this type of damage has been caused, the only cure is to carry out a complete drum renewal.

wash load.
metal drum
(raised sect
plastic foun
indicate the
similar item.

To rem
drum, remov
section HEA
either be ren

*Typical damag
damage to an
Although this
bad as the dan
previous drum
chips on the e
corrosion.*

rotate. A sign of a bad fit is
scaling/powder marks running
down the outer tub at the fitting
point. If the hose feels sticky or
tacky to the touch, it should be
replaced. **Note:** If this hose has
leaked, the water would have
contained detergent. If the water
has come into contact with the
suspension legs it may cause a
loud squeaking/grinding noise
just before and after the spin.
(This fault is more pronounced
on Hoover Automatics). This is
because the suspension works its
hardest at this time. Please refer
to the section: SUSPENSION.

If your type of washer has a
hose connected between the
outer tub and the rear of the
machine, this is called an air vent
tube. This in itself cannot leak as
no water passes through it,
although it may be used if the
machine overfoamed, overfilled or
was spun whilst still full of water.
The hose is of the grommet
fitting type, and should be
checked for perishing as before.
Most modern machines use the
soap dispenser as the air vent as
well as the water inlet, thus
eliminating an extra grommet
fitting hose in manufacture.

Box 4:

The sump hose is the flexible
hose located at the bottom of the
machine. Depending on the make
and model of your appliance, this
will be in one of two
configurations:-
(a) Linking the pump and the
tub.
(b) Linking the filter and tub,
with a separate hose linking the
filter and pump, thus creating a
trap for any foreign bodies to
prevent them reaching the pump.
Again this should be
checked for perishing and
replaced if found to be tacky or
sticky. The grommet fittings
should also be checked, as
explained in Box 3, and the clips
should be checked for tightness
as explained in the pumps
section. If the machine is of the
type with a filter, all hoses to and

IT A
FI

4 CHI
SU
HO

HO

LO
CLIF

CHEO
OUTL
HOS

HOLE

5 CHECK
THERMOS
SEAL

LEAK

N
I

from the fil
filter seal sh
defects. At
advisable to
pump as de
section.

Box 5:

The the
seal are both
the back ha
outer tub, do
make and m
An exceptio
Hotpoint fro
thermostat, l
vessel are lo
the outer tub
door seal. A
components
removal of th
machine. De
found in the
section.

Chapter 9.

Machine will not empty

Machine will not empty

Of all the faults reported, this
must be one of the most
common. Often this fault and the
'leak' fault are one of the same.
The reason for this being that on
many machines there is no 'spin
inhibit system'. This is especially
true of older machines, or
machines that are produced
abroad. If there is no spin inhibit
system, it means that if for any
reason the machine cannot
empty, it will still try to spin. The
consequence of this action, is
that the increased drum speed
pressurises the inner tub, causing
leaks from soap dispensers, air
vent hoses and door seals. Thus
one fault can cause several
problems. On most later machines
and most of the machines
currently produced in Britain, the
level switch inhibits (stops) the
machine *before* the spin if a level
of water is detected. This means
that if there is water in the
machine, the pressure causes the
switch to switch to the *off*
position, therefore not allowing
the machine to spin. For a more
detailed description of the
pressure switch, please refer to
the section: PRESSURE
SYSTEMS.

The 'not emptying' fault can
fall into three main categories.

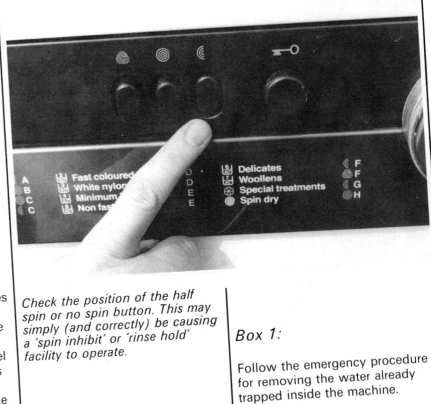

*Check the position of the half
spin or no spin button. This may
simply (and correctly) be causing
a 'spin inhibit' or 'rinse hold'
facility to operate.*

Blockage, Mechanical fault or
Electrical fault.
Please refer to the following
flowchart.

Box 1:

Follow the emergency procedure
for removing the water already
trapped inside the machine.

Box 2:

Check the outlet and sump
hoses, as well as the outlet filter
(if fitted). If a blockage or a kink
has been found, remove it and
refit the pipe(s) and filter.

MACHINE WILL NOT EMPTY FLOWCHART

Box 3:

The pump is located at the machine end of the outlet hose, and junction of the sump hose. The small chamber should be checked for blockages, the impeller should be checked for free rotation, and that it hasn't come adrift from its mounting to the pump motor shaft. If the impeller is found to be adrift from the shaft, this would give rise to no water being pumped, although the motor itself would run. A quick way to check the connection of the shaft and impeller would be to hold the shaft whilst trying to turn the impeller. If all is well they should only turn in unison. Remember to turn anti-clockwise, or the impeller will unscrew from the shaft. If a fault is found at this point, refer to the pump section.

Box 3A:

If no blockage is found in the section above, and the bearings are not suspected, the stator continuity of the pump windings must be checked. Please refer to the section: USING A METER.

Box 4:

At this point, the outlet hose should be checked again. An internal blockage such as a coin or button can act as a type of valve, and be very difficult to see. The best method of checking this is to connect the hose of a standard tap, observing the flow of water.

Box 5:

The final step is to check the wiring harness connection. Please refer to: HARNESS FAULTS SECTION.

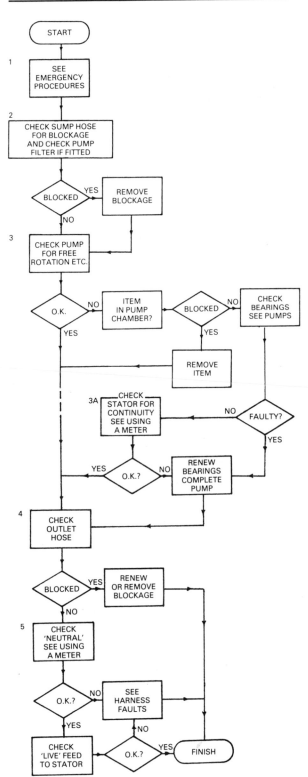

Chapter 10.

Door seal fitting

Door seal fitting – helpful hints

There are many types of door seal available, depending on make, model and the age of your machine. The removal and fitting of a 'typical' door seal is shown. The model used in this example is a Hoover machine, although the principles are the same for all machines. The door seal bridges the gap between the outer tub and the shell of the machine. This enables access to the inner drum whilst also giving a watertight seal. The seal should be renewed if found to be perished or holed at any point, paying special attention to the folds and mouldings of the door seal.

There are three ways that a door seal is secured to the outer tub and they are all very similar in concept. On the outer tub there is a 'formed lip'. When the rubber seal is located onto this lip, it is held in position by a large clamp band, and pressure is exerted by the band to create a watertight seal. The three versions of the clamp band are:-

1. A simple metal band secured by a bolt, which when tightened reduces the diameter of the band.
2. As (1), but the open ends of the band being secured by a spring.
3. This method is best described as a 'large rubber band', and is called a garter ring. When fitted correctly, the ring rests in a recess in the door seal, which in turn rests in the recess of the tub lip, therefore creating the watertight seal. Unlike the previous two methods, this band cannot be slackened by the loosening of a bolt or spring, and is best removed by prising the garter ring from its position in the seal recess by using a flat bladed screwdriver to lift it over the lip. The best way that a rubber or spring garter ring can be refitted, is to locate the bottom of the ring in the recess of the fitted door seal, slowly working the ring inside the recess in an upward direction with both hands. This can be likened to fitting a tyre onto a bicycle wheel after repairing a puncture.

Note: To aid the fitting of a door seal, a little washing up liquid may be applied to the tub lip or the door seal tub lip moulding. (Not the front lip.) This will allow the rubber to slip easily into position on the metal lip.

The fitting of the door seal to the shell of the machine is similar to the tub lip system in that three major variations are found. The most straightforward seal simply grips the shell lip with no other added support other than the elasticity of the door seal itself.

The second type also uses the shell lip, with the aid of a clamp band. A recess is formed on the outer edge of the seal for a clamp band or clamp wire to be inserted. This ensures a firm grip on the shell lip.

The third method involves a plastic flange that is screwed onto the outside of the shell. The screws that hold this flange pass through a recess in the outer front lip of the door seal, therefore securing it firmly to the front panel.

Before removing the old door seal, a simple examination of the old seal and its correct positioning will aid the renewal, as the new seal will need to fit in exactly the same position. Some door seals have a definite top and bottom, or pre-shaped sections for door hinges or catches, etc., and will fit no other way.

Remember: It is easier to line up the seal *before* fitting rather than trying to adjust the seal when the clamp bands have been fitted.

Note: Some machines have one or more of their tub weights mounted on the front section of the outer tub, encircling the door seal and tub clamp fitting, leaving little or no access to the clamp band or tub lip. Brief details of these machines are given, but greater details should be supplied with the new seal, showing the easiest way of fitting.

Early Servis machines have three metal weights bolted to the front of the outer tub, and are clearly visible when the top of the machine is removed. Careful removal of the top two weights *(only!)* will give perfect access to the tub clamp band. A point to remember on this machine is that the clamp band securing bolt will need to be removed using a socket. When removed, a slot may be cut in the head of the bolt to facilitate a screwdriver blade, therefore aiding refitting and tightening.

The procedure of removing tub weights is not necessary for Creda, Zanussi and Bendix, etc., even though they have front tub weights surrounding the tub clamp bands. The Zanussi and Creda seals can be changed through the door opening in the front panel of the machine, without removing the top at all. (Having said this, removing the

top of the machine will provide more light – remove if necessary).

Candy outer tub showing the tub weights in place around the front of the tub. The seal can be renewed with the weight in position. Bendix, Philco and Zanussi have weights completely surrounding the seal. The seal can still be renewed with these weights in position.
Some machines do not have the

large concrete weight around the front of the tub, thus allowing good access to the door seal clamp band. Hotpoint, Hoover and late Servis machines have this style of tub.
(The tub shown has been removed for the purpose of the photograph – the door seals are fitted with the tub inside the machine).
The following photographic sequences show the removal and refitting of various types of door seal.

Removal of typical door seal (Hoover)

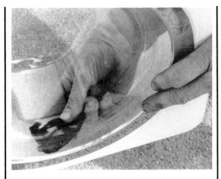

1. Check door glass inner for scale deposit ridge and clean off with non-abrasive pad.

2. Grasp door seal firmly and pull downwards to free from shell lip. Some machines may have clamp band on front lip. Remove this first.

3. When freed from lip, continue pulling in a downward direction.

4. Free complete door seal from front lip and allow seal to rest on inner side of front panel.

6. With position of clamp band and bolt in view proceed to remove band. Free seal from the clip as shown above.

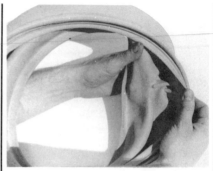

8. View showing inner lip moulding and ridge. The ridge is fitted at the 9 o'clock position when viewed from the front of the machine.

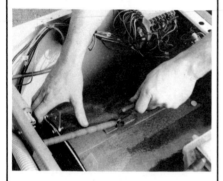

5. With top removed, free the top support springs or tie, and lean outer tub unit back as far as possible.

7. New door seal of type to be fitted to the machine shown.

9. Cutaway view of a typical door seal to show intricate moulding and positioning of tub and shell lips of the seal.

Removal of a Bendix door seal

1. Remove the plastic flanges around the door seal front.

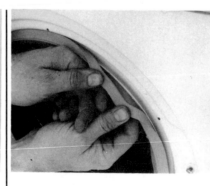

2. Remove the door seal from the front lip.

3. Showing the position of the clamp band with the top of the machine removed.

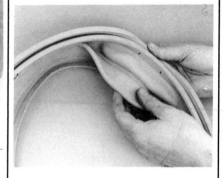

4. Picture showing the orientation of the band inside the machine. Must be re-fitted in the same position. ◄

7. New door seal checked prior to fitting and smeared with a little washing up liquid to help slide it into position. (Inner lip only). ▲

5. Slacken off tub clamp band bolt and remove old door seal.

6. View showing the tub lip and weight block gap. (Clean off any scale and/or deposit on the tub lip before fitting the new seal).

8. Ensure that the three drain holes on the door seal are fitted at the bottom of the tub lip.

Removal of a Hotpoint front loader door seal

1. Remove outer plastic surround screws, and top and bottom section.

2. Pull seal to release from shell lip, hinge and catch. ▶

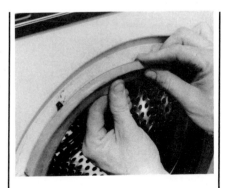

3. Unscrew the timer knob centre and remove the timer knob. Also remove the two front facia fixing screws found behind the timer knob.

4. Pull out the soap dispenser draw completely and remove the front facia fixing screws.

5. With front facia removed, remove the screws securing the front panel of the machine. ▲

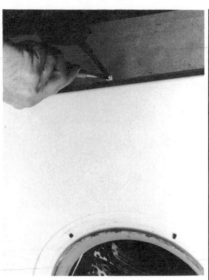

6. Four hexagonal headed screws secure the front panel under the bottom edge. (On later machines, three Philips headed screws will be found).

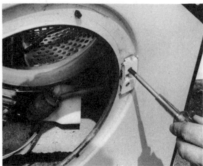

7. Remove door switch assembly and pressure switch bracket.

8. With front panel removed, the clamp band can easily be removed.

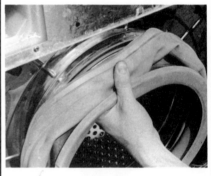

9. Note the position of hinge and catch mouldings. The door seal can then be pulled free from the tub lip.

10. When fitting a new seal to the tub lip, the tub gap can be adjusted slightly. (Note: the inner lip of the door seal is ribbed). ▶

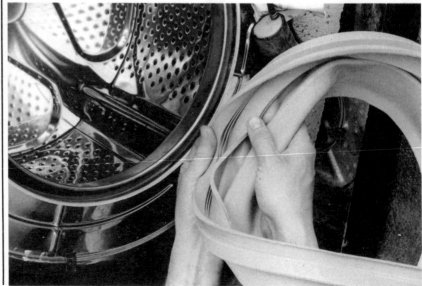

11. When the new seal is fitted in this position, check that the inner drum rotates without fouling the door seal inner. Adjust if necessary to obtain the smallest gap possible before refitting.

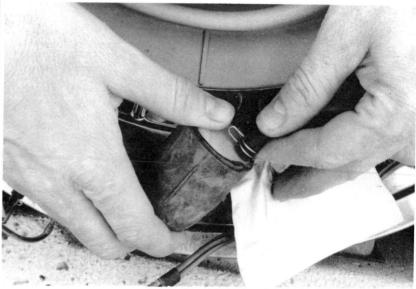

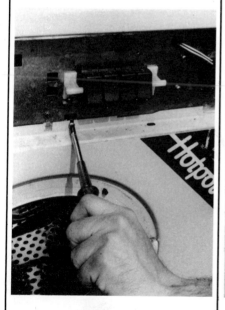

13. Refit front panel, door catch and all front panel fixings.

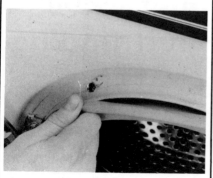

14. With front panel secured, fit the door seal to the front panel lip.

16. Refit plastic surround and ensure that the ends locate correctly. The plastic pips can be moved to aid fitting. The machine is now ready for the functional test.

12. With new door seal in this position it is wise to check that all of the leads, hoses and pressure vessel are correct before refitting the front panel. ▲

15. Lubricate the hinge and ◀ catch points with a little washing up liquid, and ease into position.

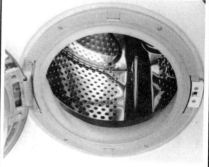

17. When fitted, the new seal should not have undue kinks or twists. It is essential that this is correctly fitted.

Chapter 11.

Inlet valves

Inlet valves

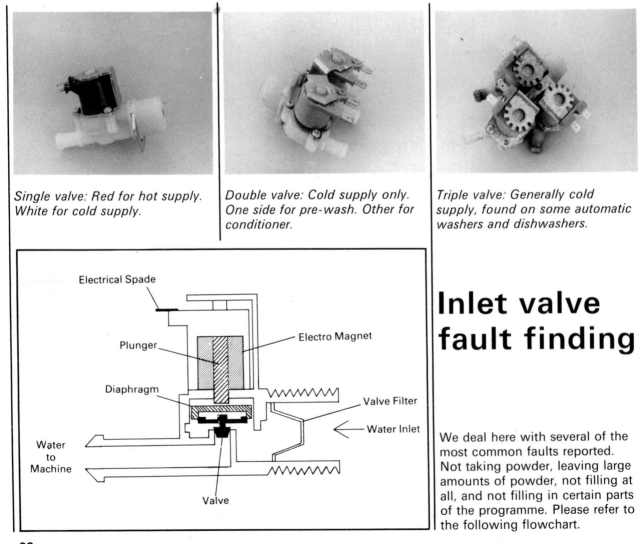

Single valve: Red for hot supply. White for cold supply.

Double valve: Cold supply only. One side for pre-wash. Other for conditioner.

Triple valve: Generally cold supply, found on some automatic washers and dishwashers.

Electrical Spade

Plunger

Electro Magnet

Diaphragm

Valve Filter

Water Inlet

Water to Machine

Valve

Inlet valve fault finding

We deal here with several of the most common faults reported. Not taking powder, leaving large amounts of powder, not filling at all, and not filling in certain parts of the programme. Please refer to the following flowchart.

Box 1

This may seem too obvious to mention, but many an engineer has been called out to find the taps were in the 'Off' position. This normally brings up the comment that the taps are "never turned off", and in this case it must have been some other devious member of the family or innocent plumber that has done the dirty deed! This comment brings in the cardinal rule that all automatic washing machines or dishwashers should be turned off at their isolation taps when the machine is not in use. This may seem a quite pointless task, but the objective is simple. If an inlet pipe should split, or an inlet valve fails to close correctly, a quite disastrous flood could occur. This would not be the case however, if the taps were turned off.

Box 2

This can be checked quite simply with the taps turned on. If a hot only wash programme is selected and the result is no fill at all, any further reference to 'the valve' in the flowchart will refer to the hot valve. If the valve allows water to pass through, select a rinse cycle. This will check the operation of the cold valve in the same way. If there is no fill with a rinse cycle, any further reference to 'the valve' in the flowchart will refer to the cold valve. The checking of a double cold valve would need a further test of the valve with the setting at the fabric conditioner or special treatments cycle, depending on the make and model of machine.

Box 3

If the main wash powder is not taken, only the centre part of the powder is taken, or if this powder is only damp, this indicates low hot water supply pressure or blocked valve filter (see valve diagram). Details will be found in the section: BASIC PLUMBING.

INLET VALVE FAULT FINDING

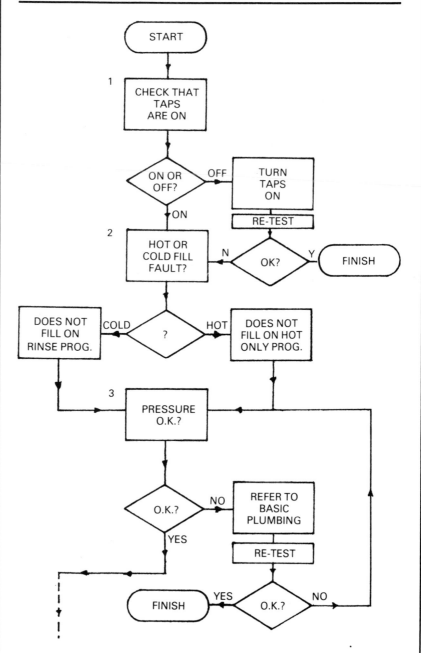

Box 4

If the heater is found to be on, when there is no water in the machine this indicates a pressure system fault, and this should be checked. Details of this process will be found in the pressure system section. If the heater is in the *off* position when there is no water in the machine, the valve would appear to be suspect. Before changing the valve, it is advisable to remove and clean the small filter found inside the valve. This can be removed by gently pulling with pliers. The valve is easily changed by removing the fixing screws and detaching the internal hose/s from the valve. Making a note of the wiring connections that are on the valve, remove them, and replace with a new valve assembly, by simply reconnecting the hoses and wires in a reverse sequence.

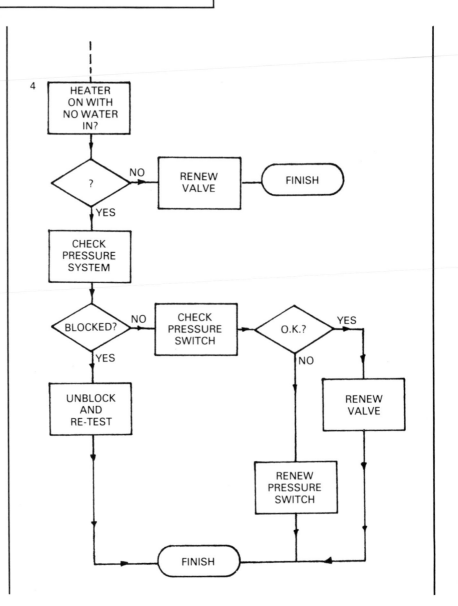

Chapter 12.

Pressure systems

The pressure system

What is a pressure system?

The pressure system governs the level of water in the machine.

Where is it located?

The pressure switch has no standard fixture location, but can usually be found at the top of the machine. It can be identified as the large circular switch that has several wires and a plastic tube attached to it. Pressure vessels have two distinct designs. The first type is an integral part of the plastic filter housing and is located behind the front face of the machine's shell, and the second is an independent unit, usually located to the rear of the machine near the tub. There is also a pressure hose system. This does the same task as the pressure vessel, although it is in the form of a flexible hose. This will either be grommet fitted to the lower part of the outer tub, or directly moulded to the sump hose.

A typical pressure switch.

How does it work?

The pressure switch does not actually come into contact with water, but uses air pressure trapped within the pressure vessel or pressure hose. When water enters the tub and the level rises, it traps a given amount of air in the pressure vessel. As the water in the tub rises, this increases the pressure of the air in the pressure vessel. This pressure is then transferred to a pressure sensitive switch via a small bore flexible tube.

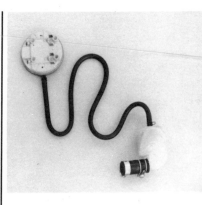

A typical pressure system.

The pressure switch is a large circular device that houses a thin rubber diaphragm, which is expanded by the corresponding pressure exerted on it. The diaphragm rests alongside a bank of up to three switches, each of which is set to operate at a different level of pressure. The switch is totally isolated from the water ensuring maximum safety.

Photograph showing the position of the pressure switch in a typical automatic. The positions may vary with makes, but all will be found as high in the machine as possible.

Showing the pressure vessel used on machines such as Hoover, Creda and Servis. ▼

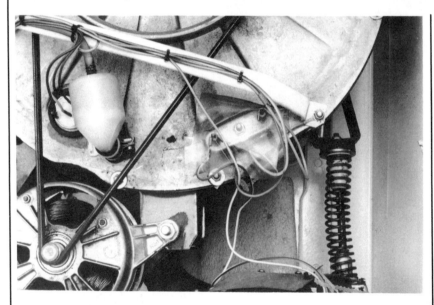

Possible faults in the pressure system

To create the highest pressure in the chamber of the pressure vessel, the vessel must be positioned as low as possible in the machine. Any sediment that is in the machine collects at this point and can therefore block the entrance. Similarly, because of its very small internal diameter, the pressure tube can also block easily. The pressure that this device creates is very small, and can easily be blocked by a very small obstruction, such as a lump of powder or sediment deposits.

The seals and hoses of the system are also of great importance. These should be checked for air leaks and blockages. Any puncture or blockage would create a loss of pressure, resulting in the wrong operation of the switches, i.e., if

Typical pressure hose.

the air pressure in the pressure vessel was to leak out, the vessel would fill with water. Thinking that the machine was now empty, the water valves would be re-energised, thus filling an already full machine. The results would be obvious.

The above example assumed that the air was stopped from getting to the pressure switch. If a blockage occurred whilst the switch was pressurised, the machine would work as normal until the machine emptied. The next time a programme was started the pressure switch would already be pressurised. Therefore the machine would not take any water, but proceed to turn the heater on. Although most heaters are now fitted with a T.O.C. (thermal overload cut-out – see Jargon), this may not act until some damage has been done to the clothes inside the drum.

Points to note

(a) The pressure system should be checked at yearly or half yearly intervals depending on the water hardness in your area.
(b) Dishwasher pressure systems are also affected in much the same way, regardless of water conditions. Fat deposits can block the pressure vessel, allowing the water level to rise to a leakage point.

(c) Any hoses or tubes that have been removed must be sealed, and any clips tightened.

(d) Blowing down the accessible end of the pressure tube may seem an easy solution to remove a blockage, but this may only be a temporary cure. Also, water may enter the pressure vessel before you can push the end of the tube back onto the pressure switch. This will render the pressure system inaccurate, if not useless.

Any loose connections on the pressure system will allow the pressure to drop. This will cause overfilling. Ensure a good seal.

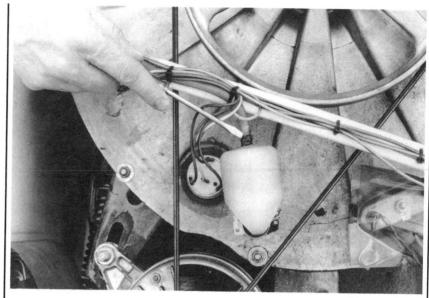

Check the pressure tube for chafing and small porous cracks. Renew if suspect. ◄

A pressure switch should only be suspected when the system has been thoroughly cleaned, checked, sealed and re-tested.

An internal view of a pressure switch, showing the diaphragm and switches. This pressure switch was faulty due to a small hole appearing in the internal diaphragm. Operation would appear correct, although the pressure would decrease during the wash, and the machine would overfill. If the first functional test was rushed, this type of fault could be overlooked. The switch in the picture, was stripped down to confirm the fault only. These switches require replacement when faulty, as they cannot be repaired. ▶

The Figure below illustrates the way a 3 level switch is used in conjunction with an economy switch, to give an alternative level as an economy feature.

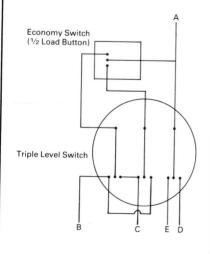

A

Economy Switch
(½ Load Button)

Triple Level Switch

B   C   E D

Checking a pressure switch

Blowing into the switch via the pressure tube, the audible ''clicks'' of the switches should be heard. This should also happen when the pressure is released. If your machine uses a single level of water, one click will be heard. Two levels of water will produce two clicks. If your machine has an economy button, a third faint click will also be heard.

Main faults within the pressure switch

(a) When the diaphragm becomes "holed" or porous. The switch can be operated and clicks heard, but will click back again without being de-pressurised.
(b) The contact points inside the switch may "weld" themselves together. This will alter the number of clicks heard, as one or more may be inoperative. Movement of the switch can free the points, although this will not be a lasting repair, as the switch will fail again.

Any of the above faults require the fitting of a new switch. The make, model and serial number of the machine should be stated when ordering, as pressure switches are internally pre-set for specific machines, although the external appearance is similar. Fitting is a simple direct exchange between the old and new.

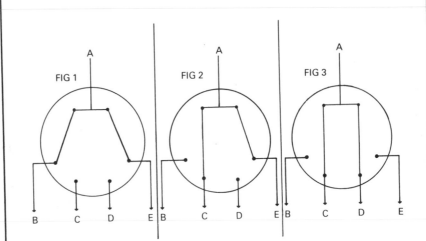

The diagram above illustrates the theoretical operation of a double level pressure switch. Fig. 1 shows the machine filling with water. If B and E are taken as hot and cold valves respectively, it can be seen that the machine is filling with both hot and cold water. In Fig. 2 the lowest level of water is reached. The pressure breaks the connection with the hot valve (B), and remakes it with the heater switch (C). The cold valve (E) continues filling. Fig. 3 shows the highest level, with the cold fill stopping, switching in the motor (D).

Clearing a pressure system blockage

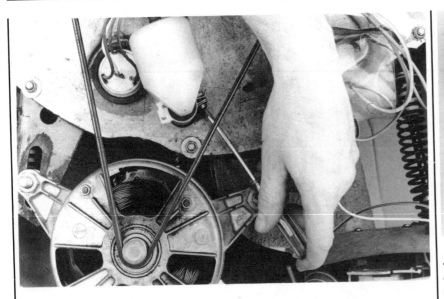

1. Note and remove all connections to the pressure switch. Remove complete system from machine.

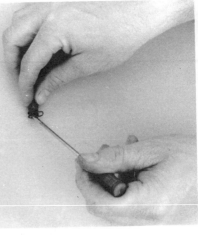

2. Check connecting hose for blockages at both ends and blow down tube to check for air leaks and to clear it of any obstructions.

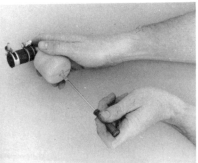

3. Clean inlet to pressure vessel and check hose for leaks and/or perishing. ◄◄

4. Carefully check outlet of pressure vessel for any build up of sludge. ◄

5. Wash out pressure vessel thoroughly to remove any loose particles and sludge.

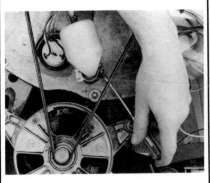

6. Check the pressure tube and any rubber hose connections for wear (i.e., rubbing on pulley, belt or clips.) ▲

A similar procedure should be followed for all types of pressure vessel and care should be taken to re-seal all hose connections that are removed. Remember to wash clear all loose particles, etc., as even the smallest of blockages in this system will cause trouble.

7. The typical position of a pressure switch on an Indesit machine. ▼

8. Pressure hose fitting on the under side of the outer tub. The grommet fitting to the tub can leak, so ensure that the good seal is maintained should the hose be removed for cleaning. ▲

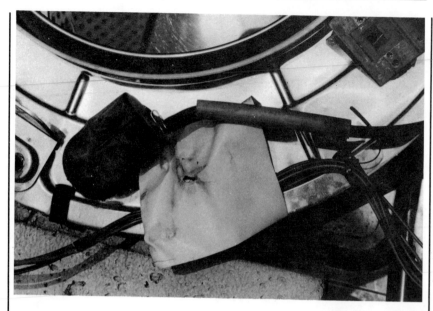

11. Integral pressure vessel and filter. These units are difficult to clean thoroughly so care is required. Also ensure a good seal on the pressure tube when refitting.

9. A front fitting pressure vessel of the type used for Hotpoint machines.

10 A pressure vessel inside a top loading machine. This vessel is held in position by a plastic nut, which is only accessible from inside the tub. This requires the removal of the outer shell and top surface. Note the sediment at the bottom of the pressure vessel. ▶

12. This picture shows a pressure vessel which is much longer than usual. Most vessels are much smaller. This type can be found in Candy and Newpol machines (pressure vessel arrowed).

Pressure switch types

1. Typical single level switch that is fitted to many basic machines.

2. Typical double level switch is more common. ▶

5. Some pressure switches may have their tube connections on the rear plate. This is only a variation on the fixing type, and does not impair the operation of the switch.

3. Typical triple level switch, which is more common on machines with plastic tubs or plastic drum paddles.

4. Variable pressure switch as fitted to Hotpoint top loader machines. The centre button changes the pressure required to operate the diaphragm. This is linked (mechanically) to the wash load select buttons on the control panel.

Chapter 13.

Pumps

Pumps

The pump is a vital part of the correct functioning of the machine and prone to various faults. Leaks from the pump may not be apparent, but the resulting pool of water usually is. So here are a few points to look out for.

Firstly check all clips on the hoses to and from the pump and tighten if they are loose.

If the leak remains, the pump's shaft seal should be checked. This is the seal that forms a water tight barrier on the rotating shaft of the motor directly between the impeller, and the front motor bearing. The seal can be broken by a collection of fluff/lint forming between the seal and the impeller itself, thus distorting the rubber seal. To check if this is happening, remove the pump chamber, by removing its securing clips or screws, and whilst securing the rotor of the pump motor, turn the impeller clockwise to undo it from the shaft, i.e., impeller and rotor are left-hand threaded. Having done this, remove any objects adhering to the shaft and refit, ensuring the pump chamber seal is in position. If the seal still leaks this will be due to it being worn or softened. On most machines, this means the

complete renewal of the pump. (Not so costly as you may think, as many genuine and proprietary pumps of good quality are now available at very low cost.

This may seem drastic for such a small seal, but the fact is that water containing detergent would have been entering the front pump bearing long before the leak was bad enough to see. This means it will probably be damaged itself and next in line to cause trouble.

The only type of pump where complete renewal can be avoided is the 'late' Hoover type, with a large flat disc type seal, that is the pump chamber seal, and the shaft seal in one. If the seal has leaked, the front bearing should be replaced at the same time as the seal. If the rotor shaft was found to be worn, (even slightly, i.e., roughness/scoured), it would probably be easier and quicker to fit a complete compatible pump, to avoid any further trouble. In fact this could be the least expensive remedy.

Other leaks can be attributable to the pump, (i.e., due to impeller damage. That is to say blades of impeller broken off or badly worn away by a solid object lodged in the pump at

sometime, e.g. small coin or tight bearings causing slow running of motor).

Both of the above will result in poor water discharge, i.e., slow draining. This in turn may cause the machine to spin whilst some water still remains, thus causing other hoses, etc., on the machine to leak or the machine to fill to too high a level, as some machines have a timed rinse fill action. On other machines, slow drainage may mean that the machine fails to spin at all. This is due to the pressure switch detecting the presence of water in the machine, (that the slow pump failed to discharge in its allotted time), therefore not allowing a spin to take place and either missing out the spin completely or stopping the wash cycle at the spin positions.

Checking the impeller and bearings can be done at the same time as checking the seal.

Most automatics are fitted with electric pumps – exceptions are the basic version of the Indesit automatics (L5, L7, L8 range). These have what is called a 'mechanical' pump.

That is to say that the pump is not a separate unit, but is attached to the rear of the main motor, and therefore runs continually in conjunction with the main motor.

This however does not mean that the machine empties when the motor runs at wash speed. Pump action only occurs on the spin speed, when the motor runs at full speed in only one direction. This means that this type of machine actually spins whilst still full of water. Good seals on door boots and all internal hoses and grommets are therefore essential to avoid leaks.

The same problems of leaks on the shaft-mounted seal are encountered on this type of pump and are even more pronounced as the pump shaft is turning for most of the wash cycle.

With leaks on this type of pump, it is essential that it should be stopped, and the fault rectified to avoid damage to the main motor.

The repair to this type of pump is quite simple. The impeller, (much larger and more solid in this case) is secured by a left-hand threaded bolt. A kit for repairing this type of pump is available with all relevant parts.

A pump that operates in a similar fashion to that of the above, is that found in the Hotpoint top-loader automatics. This is also driven by the main motor, but with this machine on wash action, the pump is used to circulate water through the top line filter/soap tray and has an 'empty only' cycle before allowing the machine to spin.

Faults found with this pump include shaft seal leaking, (this damages the bearing and allows sideways movement of the shaft and also, due to its position above the main motor, water is spread widely in the machine casing by the motor's cooling fan). Also wearing of an internal

Breakdown of Indesit manual pump.

rubber flap valve occurs. This causes the machine to empty slightly on wash cycles, thus lengthening the programme time.

This pump is a complete replacement item, and two versions are available. Large pulley drive, for early machines, and small pulley drive ($^3/_4$ inch diameter, 2 cm approximately) for late machines.

Typical electric pump with sump hose and outlet hose of the type found on many of the leading makes. The main differences with electric pumps are the pump chamber mouldings. All pumps, empty at about 8 gallons per minute.

Manual pump of this type found on Hotpoint top loader automatic.

Indesit type electric pump will fit early machines and dishwashers.

Typical pump replacement

Note: Ensure that the machine is isolated before attempting any repair on your washing machine.

In the following sequence of pictures we show the location of the pump assembly on a Hoover 1100 automatic, although it is fair to say that the pump and its location is almost standard throughout the Hoover range.

The machine was leaking badly when inspected, but was in fact still working. When questioned, the user admitted that the machine had been leaking for some considerable time, but now more water seemed to be leaking out than ever before. As you may see, this is obvious in pictures 3 & 4, by the degree of corrosion to both pump and the shell of the machine. (This level of corrosion would have been avoided by earlier detection/report of the earlier, much smaller leak.)

Shown in pictures 5 & 6 are variations of pumps that may be encountered on this type of machine. Pictures 7 to 12 show the further stripdown of the pump. In this case, it was thought best to renew the pump completely owing to the amount of water and detergent damage to both the bearings and metal laminations of the stator. (Again this would have been avoided, if the earlier leak had been dealt with sooner.)

The complete pump of the type shown in picture 6 was fitted, and the shell and mounts were coated with anti-rust compound prior to the fitting of the pump. Care must be taken that the anti-corrosion liquid does not come into contact with any rubber hoses or seals.

After replacing all hoses and connections (a simple reversal of the removal procedure) the machine was re-positioned into its correct working position and was re-connected to the water and power supply. A short rinse programme was selected to ensure that the new pump functioned correctly, to ensure that the re-positioned clips were water tight and that no other leaks were present.

At this point, the user was advised of the unnecessary danger (and damage in this case) caused by using the machine when it obviously had a fault that was ignored.

Note: In most modern machines, the pump has to be changed as a complete unit for even the smallest of problems. This is no excuse for turning a blind eye to such faults. Such behaviour is false economy.

The anti-corrosion coat mentioned can be one of many types available from DIY car centres and hardware shops. Please use as per manufacturer's instructions, taking care not to allow any contact with rubber hoses or plastics. When using anti-corrosion gel or rubber sealant indoors, care should be taken to protect the floor from spillage, and ensure that adequate ventilation is available.

2. Machine face protected and carefully laid over. Position of pump now clearly visible.

1. Ensure that machine is isolated and remove rear panel. Note location of pump – Back, right-hand corner.

3. Note and remove the hose clips and connections. Corrosion may be found on the mounting. At this point treat with anti-rust compound prior to refitting. ▶

4. Support pump whilst removing securing bolts and withdraw pump from machine.

6. This type of 'patterned' pump will fit Hoover, Creda, Servis and Hotpoint. Many other styles are available for other machines.

5. Shown are two types of Hoover pump that may be found. (Different styles of impeller and stator).

7. Lever small clips loose using small bladed screwdriver. Hold clip lightly to prevent it springing off. Screws may be found in place of clips.

8. Note pump chamber position and remove to expose impeller.

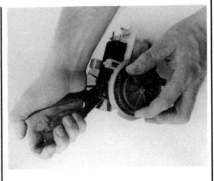

9. Whilst holding rear shaft securely, turn impeller clockwise and remove. (LH thread).

10. Rear seal exposed. In this case it is badly worn by a build up of lint upon shaft.

12. Rear view of seal showing extensive wear.

14. Secure pump firmly into position.

11. Seal removed and front bearing checked for wear and damage. Also check rear bearing.

13. When fitting a new pump as in this instance, check the bolt hole sizes of the mounting plate. On some occasions they may need enlarging.

15. Reconnect the terminals. If the pump has an earth tag, ensure that it is a good fit, as with all connections.

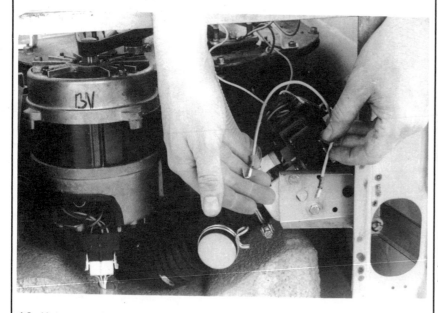

17. When the hoses and clips have been re-fitted, the machine is ready for testing on the rinse cycle. Ensure all panels are refitted before commencing functional testing.

16. If a pump has a plastic mounting plate, it is essential that the metal stator laminations are linked to the machine earth path. Make a short lead to connect the earth tag on the pump to the fixing bolt and secure firmly.

Chapter 14.

Door switches (interlocks)

Door switches (interlocks)

What is an interlock?

The word interlock is one used to describe an electrical switch behind or near the main door latching device, that is designed to give a time delay of one or two minutes, before allowing the door to be opened. The delay time differs between the makes and models of different machines.

What are the different types?

On a machine with a push/pull timer knob action, there is also a manual interlock thus giving double protection. The manual interlock system is quite straightforward, bolting or unbolting the door with the push/pull action of the timer knob, via a latching mechanism. The mechanical interlock is much the same as the electrical version except that there is no time delay.

There is one exception to the electrical interlock and that is to be found in Hotpoint automatics. These machines use a 'pecker device' to detect any drum pulley movement and do not allow entry if any movement is detected.

Philips style 3DB interlock.

Later Bendix 7TAG square interlock.

Although this is a mechanical interlock, the machine still has a microswitch on the door which does not allow the machine to run unless the door is correctly

Zanussi 3DB style interlock.

closed.

A new version of the interlock also incorporates a pressure switch type of system, that will not allow the door to open if there is any water remaining in the machine. This is a mechanical operation and will work even if the machine is unplugged. The door will only be allowed to open when the water is drained out. This must be remembered in the case of a pump failure or blockage. This system is easily recognizable due to the pressure tube leading to it.

How does it work

Due to the manufacturers' need to have their own version of

interlock, it is impossible to illustrate all of the different types, therefore, the Klixon (3DB) type of switch is used to illustrate the internal workings and theory.

The delay time is needed for the continued spinning of the drum after the motor has turned off, and is now a legal requirement. For this reason they **must not** be by-passed, as the results to small children or impatient adults **will** be disastrous.

Hoover style 1DB.

One variation of a three tag 3DB interlock (Klixon). Shown is the early Hoover 800/1100 variant.

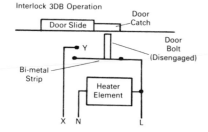

Interlock 3DB Operation

No Power to 'L', i.e. = Power therefore to 'X'.

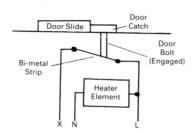

Power to 'L' heats switch therefore connects 'X' with live feed and locks the door.

Diagram (A) shows the state of the interlock before power at (L). It can be seen that the door bolt is disengaged and the bi-metal strip is in its 'rest' position. Because of this, there is no connection at point (Y), therefore no power is transmitted to (X).

Diagram (B) shows the state of the interlock when power is applied to point (L). The heater is activated, therefore heating the bi-metal strip. This then bends, engaging the door bolt and making the connection at (Y). This then allows power to flow to (X).

7 Tag 'rectangular' interlock, usually found on a Bendix machine, this can be interchanged with a 7 tag 'square' interlock.

When the power is then disconnected the heater is allowed to cool. The bi-metal strip then bends back to its rest position. This can take up to two minutes, therefore creating the delay.

Note: The heater referred to in this part of the manual is not the large heater in the drum, but is of minute proportions and is only used to heat the bi-metal strip.

Modern machines tend to link the interlock to all of the machines' other functions. If the interlock fails, power to the rest of the machine would be severed, therefore rendering the machine

useless. On older machines, interlock failure would only result in no motor action throughout an otherwise normal programme.

A two tag interlock (1DB) is shown. The 1DB being called a straight through interlock, as although locking occurs, switching does not.

The 'Rold' interlock is becoming increasingly popular with today's manufacturers. Shown is the Fagor variant. Also found in Indesit machines. ▶

Early style Indesit 3 tag 'rectangular' interlock.

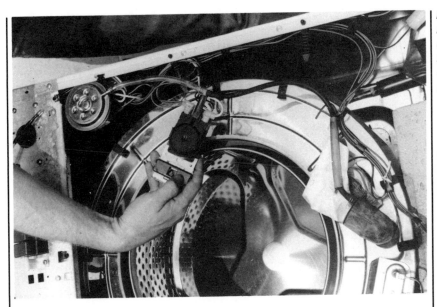

New style interlock with pressure lock included. This works in conjunction with the pressure switch, and does not allow the door to open if any water remains in the machine.

7 Tag 'square' interlock, which can be found in Bendix machines. 3 or 5 tag interlocks can also be found.

This is only a small selection of interlocks to highlight the many variations that can be encountered. Interlocks can not only change between machine manufacturers, but the models themselves may have different variants, i.e., machines with identical external appearance may have different variants of the interlock fitted.

The outer design and fitting of the interlock may change, but the function and operation differs very little between variants.

One type of interlock may be common to more than one manufacturer. It is therefore essential to obtain the correct model and serial numbers of both the machine and interlock when locating a spare part.

Chapter 15.

Thermostats

Thermostats

What is a thermostat?

In this case, a thermostat ('stat') is a device that detects the temperature of the water in the tub of the machine, and makes or breaks an electrical circuit at a pre-selected temperature. There are two main types of stat, non-variable and variable.

Where is it located?

The thermostat can usually be located on the back half or underside of the outer tub, depending on the make and model of the machine. An exception to this is the Hotpoint front loader, where the thermostat, heater and pressure vessel are located on the front of the outer tub, directly below the door seal. Access to these components is gained by the removal of the front panel of the machine. Details of this are to be found in the door seal section.

How does it work?

Diagram (A) shows a typical non variable thermostat, which can have one, two or three

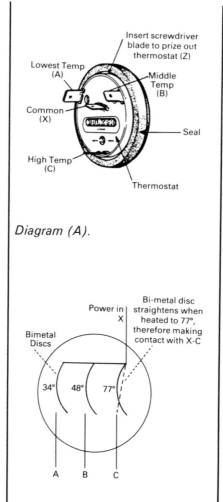

Diagram (A).

Diagram (B).

settings. Diagram (B) illustrates how a three position thermostat works. The power enters the switch at X, but cannot proceed as there is no contact. When a preset temperature is reached, the bi-metal disc set to that temperature bends, making one of the three possible contacts.

Removing and refitting a standard type thermostat – diagrams (A) & (B)

After making a note of the connections on the back, disconnect the wires from the rear of the thermostat. Insert a small screwdriver at point (Z), and prise the thermostat away from its grommet fitting. When refitting, it is advisable to smear a little sealant on the grommet to avoid leaks. Refitting is a reversal of the removal process. **Note:** Before attempting to remove or repair any component from the machine, isolate the machine from the main electrical supply by removing the plug from the wall socket.

The variable thermostat

Diagram (C) shows a pod type thermostat. This is found on machines that have a variable temperature control. Diagram (D) is a schematic diagram of the internal workings. This consists of an oil filled pod, that is connected to the switch by a capillary tube. When the oil in the pod is heated, it expands up the tube and pushes a piston. The piston acts on the switchgear, thus "breaking" one circuit and "making" the other. When the oil cools, it contracts, thus pulling the switch in the opposite direction. The switch is then in its original position and the process repeats if necessary.

Removing and refitting a pod type thermostat – diagrams (C) & (D)

The pod that will be found at the base of the capillary tube must be eased from its rubber grommet gently, taking care not to unduly kink or pull on the capillary tube itself.

Note: When fitting or refitting this form of thermostat, the capillary tube must not come into contact with any electrical contacts such as the heater terminals or moving parts such as the main drive belt. When fitted, the tube should be checked along its entire length for any possible contact with these items. Also a coiled section of at least two large turns should be left at a convenient position to absorb the movement of the tub assembly.

Testing the thermostat

The standard thermostat can be subjected to a known temperature (i.e., radiator, kettle, etc.,) and be checked with a small test meter for continuity. This process is shown in the section: USING A METER.

The pod thermostat can be tested as above, ensuring that only the pod itself is immersed in water.

Note: Whilst at room temperature, the state of the thermostat should be determined. On pod thermostats, the lowest setting must be selected. Most of the thermostats used in today's washers are normally *open circuit, making the contact* when the temperature is reached. Some, however, are normally *close circuit, breaking the contact* when the temperature is reached. If the latter of the two is found, the test meter will work in the reverse of that described in the section: USING A METER.

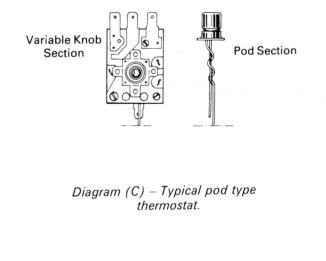

Variable Knob Section

Pod Section

Diagram (C) – Typical pod type thermostat.

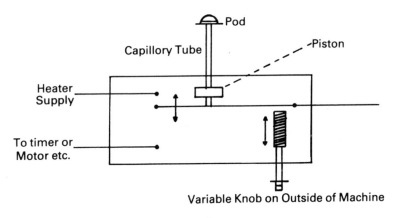

Pod

Capillory Tube

Piston

Heater Supply

To timer or Motor etc.

Variable Knob on Outside of Machine

Diagram (D) – Internal workings of pod type thermostat.

Thermostat operation flowchart

Using the following flowchart, trace the sequence of events:

1   The machine is turned on.
2   The timer impulses, fills the machine with cold water and turns the heater on.
3–4   The thermostat 'waits' until the heater has heated the water to 40°C.
5–6   When the thermostat closes (i.e., the water has reached 40°C, the timer washes for two minutes. The timer starts the washing action for two minutes. (At this point the heater is still engaged).
7–8   The above operation is repeated, again with the heater engaged. When the two minute wash has ended, the water will be at 45°C due to the extra four minute heating.
9–11   The timer then moves to the next position, which disengages the heater, and would then be ready for the programme to continue as required.
12   For the purpose of this flowchart, the wash will end here, as we are only concerned with the operation of the thermostat at this time.

Note: This is only used as an example to illustrate the use of the thermostat, and does not actually represent the way in which a wash is formed. For further information regarding the timer, see the section: TIMERS (PROGRAMMERS).

This way of using preset thermostats can give a greater variation in wash temperatures. A combination of preset and variable thermostats is common to give protection to the cooler washes, i.e., should the variable thermostat be accidentally left at 90°C and a delicate wash be selected, the preset stat would override the variable stat, therefore giving some protection to the wash.

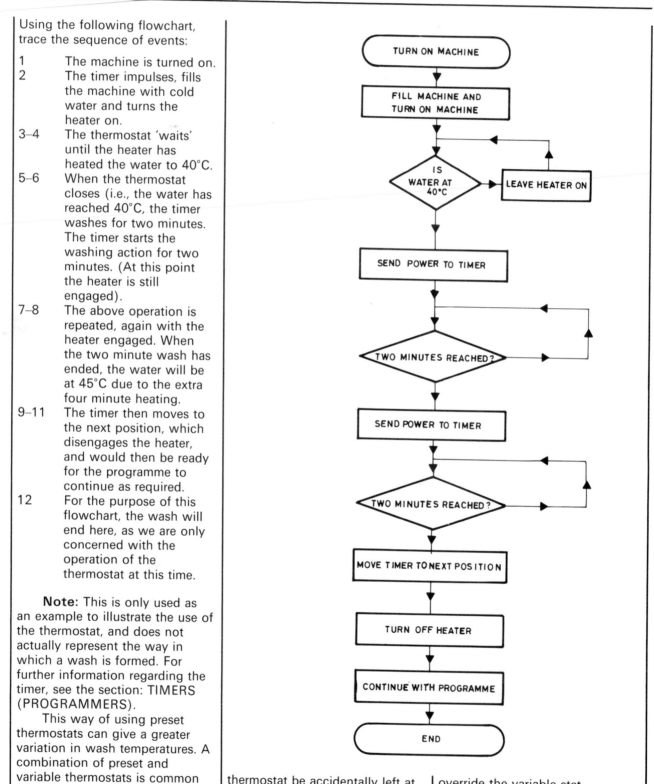

Variations

Circular 'three' step thermostat
with temperature settings marked
on outer edge. ▲

*Variable thermostat showing the
switches, capillary tube and pod.*

*Smaller two step thermostats,
found on Zanussi, Fagor and
Bendix, etc.* ◄

The above thermostats show a
small selection of those used by
manufacturers of washing
machines. All types are used
directly or indirectly to control
wash temperatures. This means
that they turn 'off' the heater as
soon as a pre-selected
temperature has been reached, to
allow the timer to advance or a
timed heat cycle to commence.

Chapter 16.

Heater

Heater

Where is the heater located?

The heater is usually located in the lower part of the tub assembly, and can be either fitted through the back half of the tub or through an aperture in the tub base itself. An exception to this is the Hotpoint front loader, where the heater is located on the front of the outer tub, directly below the door seal. Access is gained by removing the front panel of the machine. Details of this are to be found in the DOOR SEAL section.

Removal and refitting of the heater

After making a note of the connections and removing them, the heater can be withdrawn from its position by slackening the centre nut, and gently easing the rubber grommet free from its position with a flat bladed screwdriver. Refitting is a reversal of these instructions, although a little sealant should be applied to both surfaces of the grommet fitting. Care should be taken that the centre nut is not overtightened, as this would cause a distortion of the metal plate. On most automatic washing machines, the inner of the outer tube has a raised flange that engages the curved section at the end of the heater. It is important that this is located correctly when refitting the heater.

Common faults with heaters

One of the most common faults with the heater is that of open circuit, i.e., no current flows through the heater, therefore no heat is produced, and the machine will fail to move off the wash programme as the impulse via the thermostat will not be produced. This can be due to a broken or loose connection to one of the heater terminals. This then overheats, leaving an obvious discoloration of the connection or terminal, resulting in a break of the circuit at that point. Alternatively, the break in the circuit can occur within the element itself. This can be tested for continuity, as described in the section: USING A METER.

Another fault that can occur is that of low insulation. In this case please refer to the section: LOW INSULATION.

Accompanying the low insulation fault is that of the short circuiting of the heater, caused by a complete breakdown of insulation. This results in the machine blowing fuses.

Should any of the above faults occur, a complete replacement of the component is required. This is so even for the double element heaters. If one of the two elements should fail, a complete element replacement is needed.

Modern machines that have plastic or nylon tubs are now fitted with overheat protectors. These are essential and are linked in line with the live feed to the heater. They are fitted for safety reasons, for if a pressure switch or pressure system were to fail, it is possible for the heater to be engaged with no water in the tub.

In a machine with a metal tub, this would be most unwelcome, but only minor damage to the clothes would be caused. If this were to happen in a plastic/nylon tub, the result can be extremely dangerous.

Note: Under no circumstances should the overheat protection be removed or bypassed.

The overheat protector that is used on Philips machines is an integral part of the heater and is similar to a capillary thermostat switch. Conversely, Hotpoint uses a separate protector that is available as a renewable item.

If such items are faulty, this would give rise to no heating of the wash water and would also cause the machine to 'stop', i.e., fail to move through the programme.

If this item is found to be 'open circuit', check the pressure switch and system prior to renewing the overheat device.

A few of the many variations of heaters

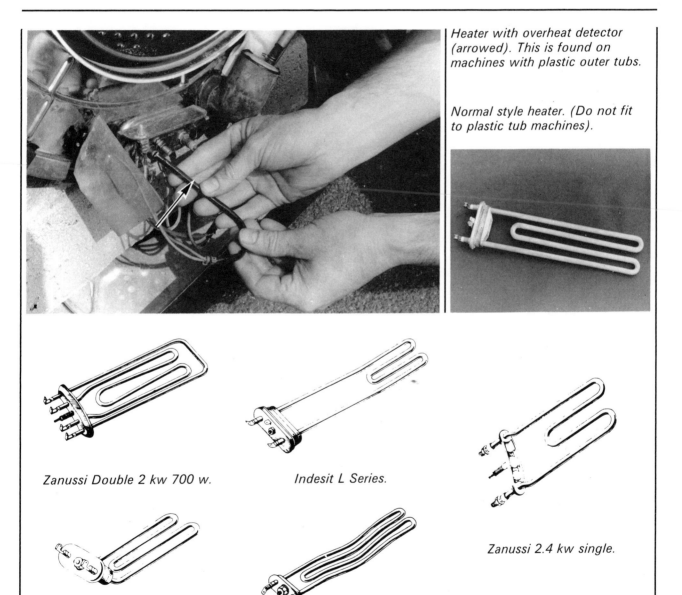

Heater with overheat detector (arrowed). This is found on machines with plastic outer tubs.

Normal style heater. (Do not fit to plastic tub machines).

Zanussi Double 2 kw 700 w.

Indesit L Series.

Zanussi 2.4 kw single.

Bendix 2 kw also Philco 2 grommet size available.

Candy Type.

Chapter 17.

Suspension

Suspension

What is the suspension?

The suspension is the system that controls all of the movement of the washer when it is in use. Without the suspension, or when damaged, the machine would move violently when in use.

What different types of suspension are there?

The spring type suspension, which is simply a strong spring.
   The damper and spring suspension which is not unlike the system in motor cars.
   The friction damper, which consists of two arms gripping a metal plate tightly, therefore slowing down the movement of the tub.

How can faults be avoided?

The main fault to check for is that the guides can wear, allowing the shaft to jump out of position, and the top rubbers to soften or wear. This allows a condition called 'twisted tub' to occur. This is because the suspension on one side of the tub is not correctly positioned, therefore allowing one side of the tub to bang on

the side of the shell and damage the tub. A noise fault may also become apparent at the top of the suspension, caused by soapy water seeping into the suspension via the dispenser or dispenser hose. This is best removed by a spray of lubricant/moisture repellent. The top and the guides of the suspension are the only parts that should be lubricated. When fitting top rubbers, the machine should be laid on its face, and the suspension should be held tightly with grips at the top end only. The nut can now be undone. *Do not hold the bottom of the shaft as the marks will wear the plastic guides.*

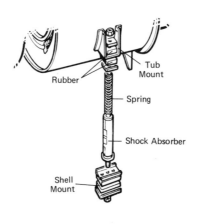

LARGE DAMPER & MOUNTS

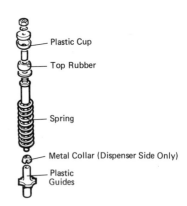

SPRING ONLY UNIT HOOVER TYPE

Friction damper suspension systems

The friction damper system

The friction damper is not unlike the disc braking system on a motor car. Two rubbers with asbestos pads are mounted on two spring steel arms. These rest either side of the flat plate attached to the tub. Should the tub then move, the action is slowed down by the friction of the pads against the plate. This is a very cheap, very effective form of suspension.

When this type of damper is worn, the tub will move excessively and possibly emit a squeaking noise. The noise will be caused by the rubber pad mounts coming into contact with the moving plate, due to the asbestos material being worn. This is easily overcome by the renewal of the pads themselves. After isolating the machine it should be laid on its back to enable the steel spring arms to be opened. When opened, the pads can be prised from their ball and socket joint.

Note: If the pads on this system become glazed and/or shiny on their contact faces, this will cause a "chattering" noise. To avoid renewal, roughen the faces up with sandpaper and refit. If unsuccessful, the pads will have to be renewed.

Do not under any circumstances put oil or grease on friction damper systems. Do not inhale the dust from the friction pads as this can be harmful to the lungs.

The damper and spring system

The damper type system is similar to the shock absorbers on your car, and they do the same job. If the smaller version of the system is used, the tub will not actually rest on the damper, but will be hung from springs at the top of the tub, using the dampers at the bottom for shock absorption only. In the larger systems however, the tub is held only by much larger dampers at the bottom of the tub, with retaining straps at the top to limit sideways movement.

Faults found with this type of solid damper will have the same symptoms of the friction damper system. The only remedy in this case is the complete renewal of the faulty damper. This can be done by laying the machine onto its face, taking the usual care and isolation procedures. Access to the dampers can be gained by removing the back panel, and unbolting the damper from the shell mount. **Do not remove the top springs or straps.**

Friction type damper.

The spring only system

The spring only system is found on Hoover machines. The spring or the mounts can be changed separately if required or replaced as a complete unit.

Note: The left and right springs are usually of different ratings. Be sure to specify the required size when obtaining a replacement. Also, two small springs are used for sideways support, and these may have come out of position. Whilst carrying out this type of repair, these small springs may become disconnected. They must be refitted correctly. Please examine the positions of these springs before you start.

Note: It must be stressed that any combination of these systems can occur. A damper system may complement a spring system, or a spring system may complement a friction damper system. Please read *all* sections thoroughly before starting any repair on the suspension system.

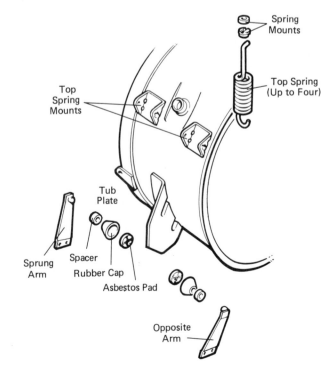

Spring Mounts

Top Spring (Up to Four)

Top Spring Mounts

Tub Plate

Sprung Arm

Spacer

Rubber Cap

Asbestos Pad

Opposite Arm

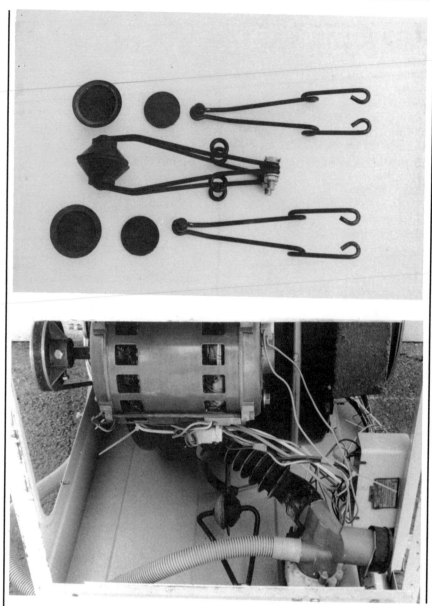

Indesit friction damper that shows the spring steel arms clearly. These support the rubber mounts with friction pad inserts.

A friction damper system from a Fagor machine. This is viewed in situ, as the complete front panel can be removed. The front panel removal can be achieved easily by removing the lower panel and two securing screws.

1. View of spring and slide suspension. This is prone to softening of the rubber mount at the top of the suspension leg. ▼

Friction damper systems consist of up to four large springs that support the tub from the top, whilst also allowing movement. This movement is then 'damped' (restricted) at the bottom of the tub by the friction pads that are located either side of the 'tub plate'.

Note: If the top springs are removed, mark them so as to ensure that they are replaced in the same order. This is because the length and tension for the springs may differ for each position.

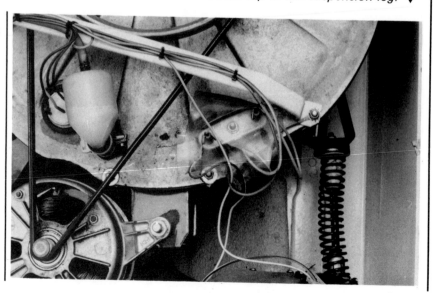

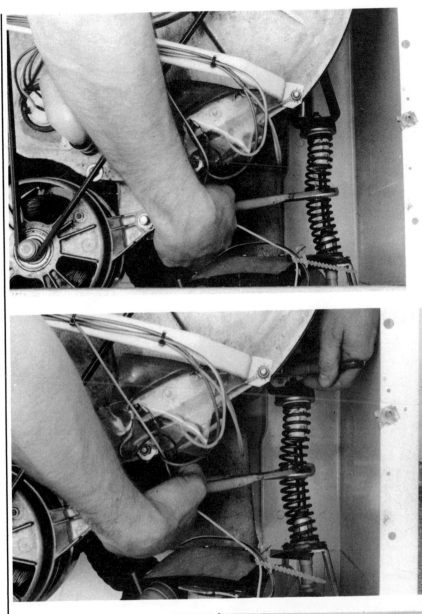

2. To renew the top rubber, the whole unit will have to be withdrawn. Grip the shaft through the spring at the top only, using adjustable pliers inserted through spring.

3. Whilst gripping the metal shaft tightly, the securing nut can be removed. (Right hand thread). Note the correct assembly of parts and pull spring downwards to remove top bush.

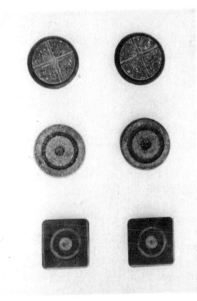

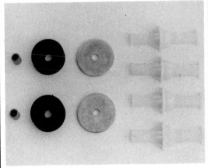

4. New set of rubber sleeves and spacer washers. Do not be tempted to renew one side only – you must renew both sides!

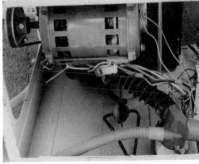

5. Friction style damper. Access is much easier with hoses removed. Do not lubricate this type of suspension.

6. Friction pads from various machines. Top section is pad and mount for Zanussi, middle section pad for Indesit, and lower is square pad for Candy.

Chapter 18.

Timers (programmers)

Timers (programmers)

The programmer (or timer, as it is more commonly known,) is the unit located at the top of the machine, directly behind the selector knob.

When a programme is selected, the timer follows a pre-determined sequence switching components in and out (i.e., heater, pump, valves), for various lengths of time. Due to the apparent complexity of this component, it wrongly tends to be regarded as a 'no go' area.

The intention of this manual has been to show that the automatic washing machine is not so mysterious, and when broken down into its constituent parts, its simplicity of operation is revealed. To describe the workings of the timer in your washer, we would need to know the make, model number, date of manufacture and the timer number itself. These are needed to ascertain which variation of timer and associated variation of programmes that your particular machine has. In their most infinite wisdom, the manufacturers have seen fit to change their timers, numbers and wiring colours, etc., with regularity.

For instance the Hoover automatic in the last ten years has seen at least fourteen basic models in this time, but at least twenty six variations of timer and no less than thirty different wiring diagrams. The other manufacturers are no different. The story is much the same had we selected Hotpoint, Bendix or any other manufacturer, yet the machine's other internal parts have changed very little in that period. As you can see, to give detailed information about the unit that is in your particular machine, a book several times the size of this one would be needed. What follows is a general description of how timers work, some of the most common faults and their symptoms.

How a Crouzet timer works

What follows is a description of how a Crouzet timer works. This is one of the most common timers and is found in more than fifty per cent of the machines sold in Britain today. The Crouzet is an edge cam timer, which means that each switch within the timer is operated by its own cam on a central rotatable barrel.

This allows switches to be dropped or lifted into different positions at the same time. This operation can be linked to that of the old style piano or musical box that played a tune with the aid of a cylinder. If the cylinder were to be changed, a different tune would be produced. The same principle applies to the timer. Although the external appearance of the timer does not change, a simple change of the central barrel will give the manufacturer different switching sequence and therefore a different machine to put on the market. Because of this, when changing the timer it is important that the correct version is used, i.e., one with the same central barrel. This is shown by the serial number on the timer.

On the central barrel there are several cams, with each cam having two corresponding switches. The barrel is rotated by the cam advance motor, which is energised by impulse commands such as that from the thermostat, i.e., if the selected temperature is reached, the thermostat closes, thus causing the motor to run. The motor will continue to run until a cam position is reached that breaks the impulse path (motor circuit). The barrel is now in the correct position for the next sequence of instructions.

The Crouzet is normally a 45 step cycle. This means that on one complete revolution of the cam, it will have initiated 45 switches (45 'clicks'). A variation to this, is one of 60 step cycles. These are usually found when half of the timer cycle is for robust washes and long spins, and the remaining section given to cooler washes and short/delicate spins, i.e., letters A – F on the selector knob for hot wash, rinse and long spin and G – K for delicate wash, rinse and short spin.

Next to the advance motor is the timing motor, which times all of the functions of the machine, i.e., washing, spinning, etc. The timing motor drives a timing cam which, via internal gearing, turns one revolution every two minutes. Therefore a six minute wash consists of three – two minute timing requests.

Another function of the timing motor is that it reverses the main motor on the wash action cycle. This is done by continually rotating two cams, on which two sets of switches are located. The combination of which are used depending on the type of wash selected, i.e., if a delicate wash is selected, the motor is told to rotate for five seconds clockwise, pause for fifteen seconds, then rotate for five seconds anticlockwise. The cam does this by lifting the switches into three positions, ON, OFF, REVERSE. Delicate and heavy washes can be achieved by using different configurations of the same sequence, i.e., a heavy wash could be made up of the sequence:- Wash for fifteen seconds clockwise, pause for five seconds, and wash for fifteen seconds anticlockwise. The times of fifteen and five seconds are not random choices, but are directly proportional to the two minute timing cycle.

Cams operate similarly for the other switches in the timer. For example, at the correct point

Typical Crouzet timer.

in the programme, the cam on which the heater switch rests will allow the switch to make contact, therefore engaging the heater. The cam will also engage the correct thermostat switch for that programme. When the correct heat is reached and the timer has timed out, the thermostat then impulses the cam advance motor. In English, this is read as "When the temperature is reached, finish timing and then impulse (move) onto the next cam position".

Internal view of cam barrel. Each row is for one switch block and has three levels.

Internal view of switch bank. Note switch movements and cam position (Crouzet timer).

Crouzet timers have either a large code number on the top of the timer or a smaller, longer number on the left hand side. When ordering a new item all numbers that are on the timer should be quoted together with the make, model and serial number of your machine.

An alternative to the two motor Crouzet, is the one motor version, where the one motor does both of the jobs via the cams. This version is common in the Creda automatics.

With a little imagination, it should be quite clear how a programme actually works; not by some mysterious phenomenon, but by a sequence of simple movements that combine to form a complete operational programme.

How a face cam timer works

The same basic principles apply as in the Crouzet unit only the switches are operated by an etched disc that allows the switches to drop in and out of the recessed positions on its face. Face cam timers are of the one motor variety.

The timers are easily identifiable by the fact that an edge cam timer is much longer or deeper than the face cam. This is because the face cam timer is much slimmer due to the fact that only one disc is used to operate all of the switches.

The main drawbacks of timers

(a) Units cannot be repaired. Complete unit changes are needed for timer faults. (Some Crouzet timer motors can be obtained as spares. Ensure correct rotational direction required by turning centre.)
(b) Without detailed information of the switching sequences of the faulty timer, faults are very difficult to trace, as a combination of switches may be used.
(c) Units can often be difficult to fit. (Unless a logical approach is used!)

The main benefits of timers

(a) Modern timers are very reliable.

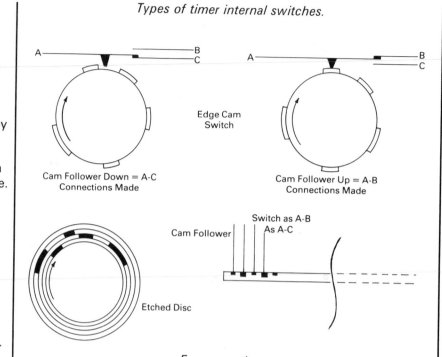

Types of timer internal switches.

Edge Cam Switch

Cam Follower Down = A-C
Connections Made

Cam Follower Up = A-B
Connections Made

Cam Follower

Switch as A-B
As A-C

Etched Disc

Face cam timer.

(b) New units are relatively low in cost.

It must be remembered that when a fault is suspected, it is not always the most complicated component that can cause the most trouble. If a process of elimination is used and all other parts of the machine are found to be working correctly, it is only then that the timer should be suspected. (Unless of course in the case of obvious failure, such as a burn out or damage to the timer).

Fitting hints

Note: Ensure that the power is turned off and that the plug is removed from its socket at all times. Do not remove the timer from the machine at this point.

The removal and subsequent exchange of the timer is a long and tedious task, and should not be undertaken lightly.

Do not remove any wiring as yet, but thoroughly check for any overheating of the connections to and from the timer spades (connections), i.e., if a fault is suspected in the heater switch, trace the wire from the heater to the timer. This gives the location of the heater switch, and should be examined for any signs of burning or being loose. (This would at least confirm your suspicions.)

Having decided that the timer is at fault, a note should be taken of all of the numbers that are on the timer, together with the make, model and age of your machine.

Armed with this information, you can obtain an *exact* replacement.

When the replacement has been obtained, visually check that they are identical, as timers will not be exchanged by any known company, once they have been fitted. (You have been warned!). Having confirmed that it is the correct replacement, and the accompanying documents have been read thoroughly, you can proceed to swap the wiring. The only way that this can be done is by placing the new timer in the same plane as the original, swapping the wires on a one-to-one basis. (Although very time consuming, this is by far the safest method.) A mistake at this point would be almost impossible to rectify without a wiring and timer diagram, therefore it is advisable to ask a colleague to supervise operations. When all connections have been successfully exchanged, the timer can be fitted into position, ensuring that any interlock parts (parts that connect to door latches), are positioned correctly. Once fitted into position, and the covers have been refitted, the power can be turned on, and a test programme can be implemented.

Note: Some timers have small metal clips that join/link terminals together, these do not come with this new timer. Ensure they are swapped from the original.

Timer variations

The timers shown are a small selection that are used in today's automatic washing machines.

A manufacturer may have numerous variations of the same timer. For instance, although your timer may be a Crouzet, your neighbours may have the same machine, with seemingly the same timer in it. This may, in fact, be a variation of the same timer.

These variations are identifiable by the slight difference in serial numbers shown on the timer. This illustrates the need to obtain the exact number of your timer and machine when a replacement is to be obtained.

Typical face cam timer (terminals on rear).

Bendix face cam (Eaton timer).

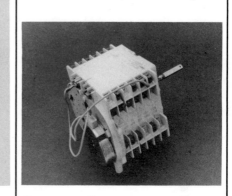

One motor Crouzet type to fit Creda.

Shown is one of the easiest types of timers to replace. This type has Duotine block connectors and not single tags. Some later edge cam timers may be able to accept block connectors instead of tags. This makes timer removal and refitting a great deal easier.

Indesit edge cam timer.

Chapter 19.

Low insulation

Low insulation

What is low insulation?

Low insulation is best described as a slight leak to earth, of the wiring of one or more of the components in the machine. If very slight, this will not harm the machine, but will be an indication of faults to come.

What does it do?

Low insulation is a slow breakdown of the insulating properties of a normally electrically leakproof system.

How is it caused?

This can be caused by normal wear and tear over a long period. For instance in the motor, a build up of carbon deposits will result from the normal wearing of the motor brush. This slowly lays down a conductive layer of carbon dust from the brush (which is a current carrying connection), to the metal body of the motor (earthed metal). In this case early detection of such low insulation, would mean that the motor could be cleaned to rid it of these deposits before a fuse was blown. If left in its 'dirty'

state, damage would almost certainly occur to the motor and module. This condition should be tested for after leaks, etc., as any conductor of electricity can cause low insulation. Water is a conductor of electricity. Carbon deposits are only one form of low insulation in the motor, another cause being the natural breakdown of the normally insulated windings. This fault would not be cured by cleaning, and would require a renewal of the failed part.

How can it be detected?

When an engineer tests for low insulation, he will use a device called a metrohm/low insulation tester. The law requires repair engineers to test for low insulation, and there is a minimum allowable level.

The law requires that these tests are made by commercial repair engineers:-

Between the earth pin on the plug and all earth connection points within the machine, the maximum resistance should be 1 ohm, i.e., no resistance – a perfect connection.

With the machine turned on, select a wash programme. Between the live pin on the plug and the earth pin on the plug, the minimum resistance should be 1 megaohm, i.e., very high resistance – no connection at all.

Repeat this test between the neutral and the earth pins of the plug.

Repeat the above test, setting the machine to a spin programme.

It is an unfortunate fact that many engineers do not possess such a device, and therefore do not check for low insulation.

This does not mean that you should not.

A meter to test for low insulation would cost upwards of one hundred pounds, and is therefore out of the reach of most D.I.Y. people. A cheap alternative is an in line circuit breaker. The appliance is plugged into the circuit breaker, which is then plugged into the socket. The purpose of the device is to detect low insulation or leakage to earth and turn off the power to the appliance. Another advantage with this device is that it can be used in other places where low insulation could be dangerous, i.e., Lawnmowers, irons, etc. In our opinion circuit breakers are invaluable for home safety of all electrical appliances.

Points to remember about low insulation

Ensure that any disconnection or removal of wires is safe, and not earthing via another wire or the shell of the machine, etc.

Whilst disconnecting any wires during the testing of low insulation, it should be remembered that the machine must be isolated from the mains at all times, and the panels must be replaced before the machine is re-tested.

Before testing for low insulation using a circuit breaker, all earth paths of the machine should be tested. This is done by connecting a meter between the earth pin of the plug, and all other metal parts of the machine in turn. Maximum resistance should be 1 ohm. See section: USING A METER.

Testing for earth using an ammeter. Note that in picture A, the door hinge is used, and in picture B, the door slide is used in this instance.

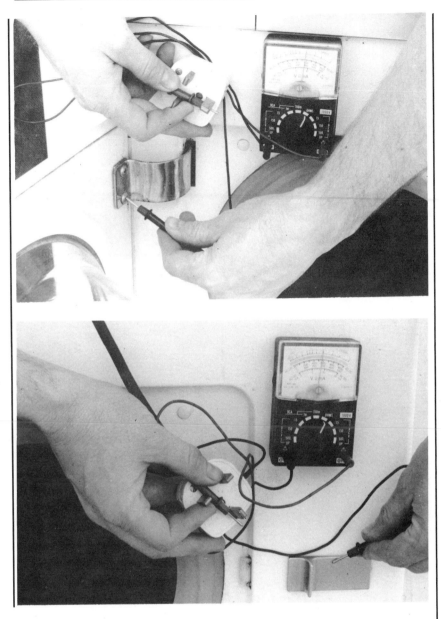

Low insulation flowchart overleaf

LOW INSULATION FLOWCHART

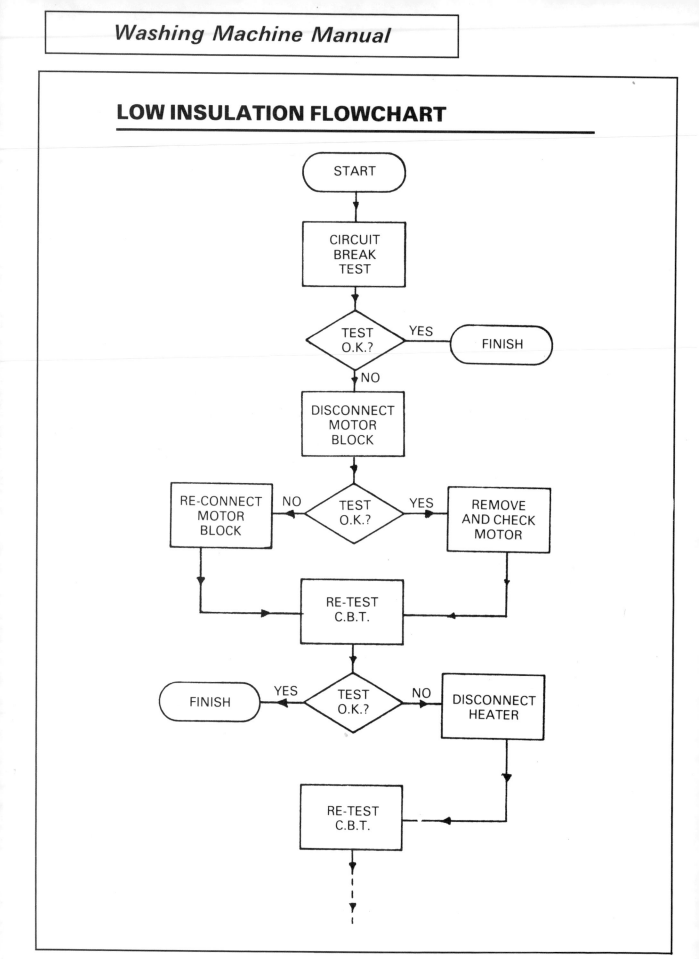

START

CIRCUIT
BREAK
TEST

TEST
O.K.? — YES → FINISH

NO

DISCONNECT
MOTOR
BLOCK

RE-CONNECT
MOTOR
BLOCK ← NO — TEST
O.K.? — YES → REMOVE
AND CHECK
MOTOR

RE-TEST
C.B.T.

FINISH ← YES — TEST
O.K.? — NO → DISCONNECT
HEATER

RE-TEST
C.B.T.

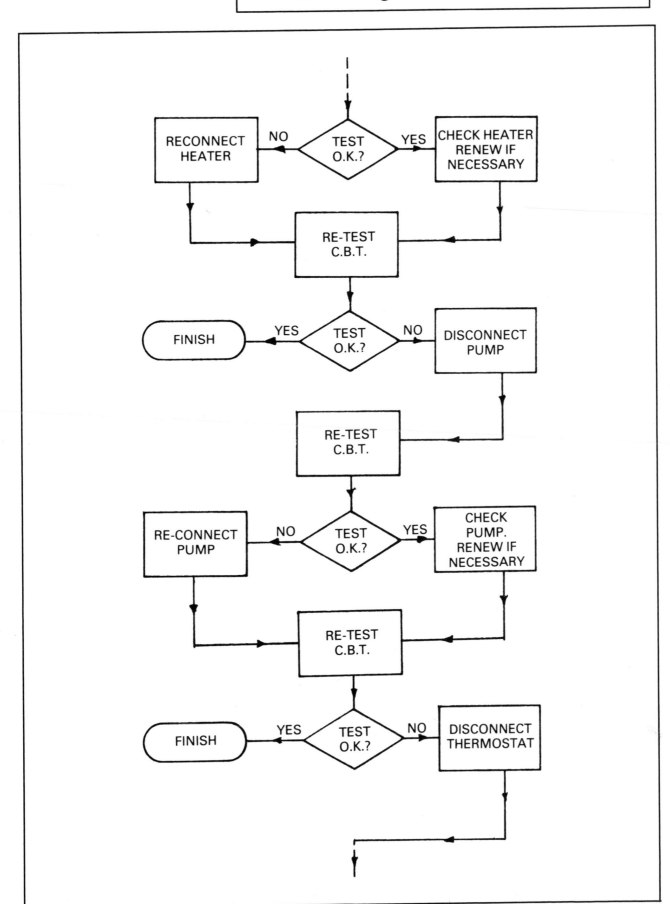

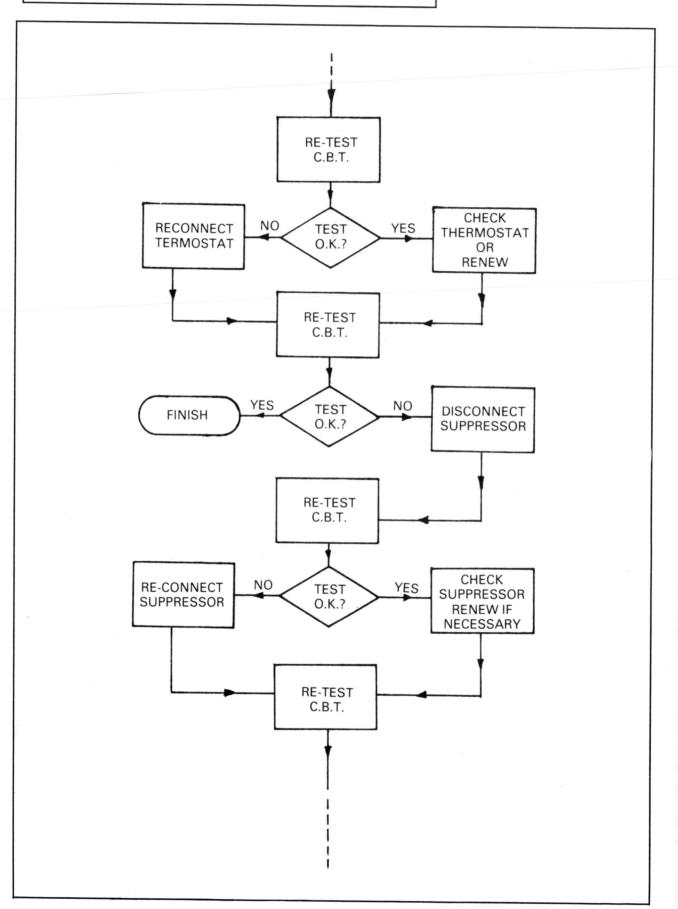

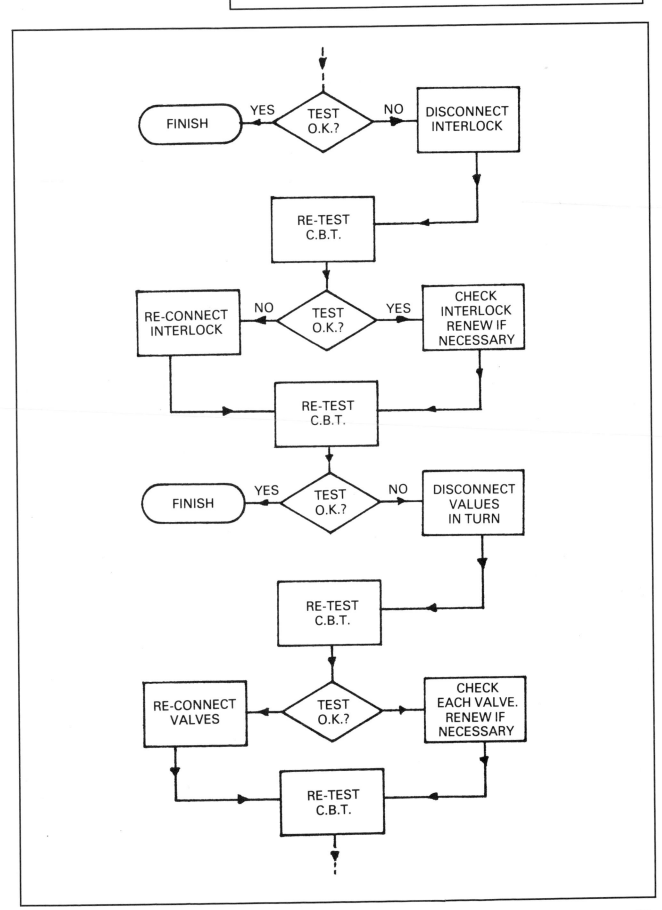

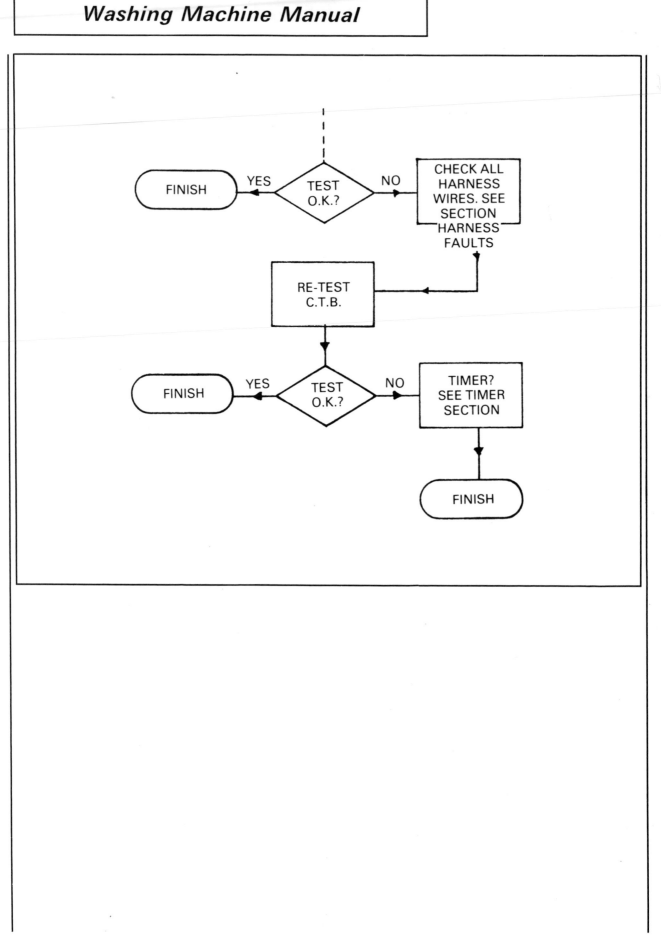

What is an RCCB (residual current circuit breaker)

RCCB's, previously known as earth leakage circuit breakers (ELCB's), are firmly established around the world as the primary means of providing protection against electrocution and fires caused by electrical faults. Less than $1/4$ amp leaking to earth from faulty installation can generate sufficient heat to start a fire or, if leaking through a human body for only $1/20$ second, can cause heart fibrillation and subsequent death.

How an RCCB works

An RCCB protects by constantly monitoring the current flowing in the live and neutral wires supplying a circuit or an individual item of equipment. Under normal circumstances, the current flowing in the two wires is equal but, when an earth leakage occurs due to the fault or an accident, an imbalance occurs and this is detected by the RCCB which automatically cuts off the power in a split second.

To be effective, the RCCB must operate very quickly and at a low earth leakage current. Those most frequently recommended are designed to detect earth leakage faults in excess of 30mA ($3/100$ths of an amp) and to disconnect the power supply with 30ms ($3/100$ths of a second); these limits are well inside the safety zone within which electrocution or fire would not be expected to occur.

The use of the 'B & R' RCCB in this book is to aid those who do not possess a low insulation test meter. This is a piece of equipment that should be owned and used by every competent electrical engineer, but is outside the price range that can be paid by the average Do It Yourselfer.

The RCCB units shown were kindly provided by B & R Electrical Products Ltd., of Templefield, Harrow, Middlesex. The units manufactured by B & R are made to the highest possible standards and are available at most good electrical retail outlets and D.I.Y. stores, etc.

It must be remembered that the units have a wide range of uses, and can not only be used in the manner that we use them in this book. RCCB's are designed to ensure safety when using things such as lawnmowers (where there is a danger of cutting through the cable), irons, washing machines, etc., (where water and electricity are in close proximity).

RCCB's are designed to sever mains current should your electrical appliance malfunction, or should you cut through the mains cable of your lawnmower for instance. They are not designed to let you increase the risk to yourself; they are simply a fail safe device and should be used as such. In our opinion, used correctly they are an invaluable asset to your household.

Adaptor RCCB useful for its portability. An essential item for all households.

Standard style single RCCB socket.

New style double socket RCCB for use in home or workshop.

Chapter 20.

Electric motors

Electric motors

There are two types of electric motors used in today's automatics, the brush motor and the induction motor.

Where is the motor located?

With the rear panel removed from the machine, the motor will usually be bolted to the underside of the outer tub. The exception to this is the Hotpoint front loader where the motor can be found bolted to the top left hand side of the outer tub.

Brush motors

This consists of two sets of electromagnets. An outer fixed set called the field coil, and an inner free set called the armature. The armature is made up of many separate windings. It is configured in such a way that power is only supplied to one set of windings at a time. The corresponding movement induced in the armature, continuously brings a new set of windings into circuit, whilst the previous winding circuit is broken. The windings are continuously out of synchronization, therefore inducing continuous rotation of the armature whenever power is supplied. Reversal of the motor is simply by reversing the power flow through the field coil winding, via a set of reversing switches in the timer. This type of motor can be used with alternating current (a/c) from the mains, or with direct current (d/c) from a battery. This type of motor is often used for the main drive motor, especially on British machines.

Induction motors (capacitor start)

This type of induction motor has a capacitor to 'kick' the rotor into action by putting a delay into one of the motor's windings. The motor is then unbalanced, therefore causing rotation in the direction of the start winding. A reversal of power in the start winding reverses the motor. Speed is governed by the number of windings supplied with power.

Induction motors (shaded pole)

This type of motor is associated with pumps and low power fans, etc., as it has low starting torque, i.e., this type of motor is impeded from starting easily, as the initial rotation is only from copper segments bound into the stator. When power is applied to the stator coil, the copper segments create a permanent imbalance in the magnetic field produced. This induces rotational movement.

Brush motors in greater detail

A brush motor can be readily identified by its shape, as its length is greater than its width. Due to a switching device, a brush motor can be used either with a/c from the mains or d/c from a battery. The switching device is called the commutator, and is made up of many copper segments. Each segment is connected to a winding in the armature and is supplied with electricity through two stationary pieces of graphite, called brushes. These are pushed onto the commutator by springs.

When power is applied to the motor, current flows to the field coil and through the brushes to the commutator. This magnetises the armature coils inducing rotation. As the armature rotates, the next two segments of the commutator come into contact with the brushes. This operation is repeated many times per second.

Speed control of this type of motor is achieved by 'pulsing' the power to it, i.e., if the pulse is slowed, the motor slows. This is not as straightforward as it may seem, as the pulse has to be smooth to eliminate any jerky action at low speeds. This is achieved by the module which is dealt with in the section: MODULE CONTROL IN BRUSH MOTORS.

Main drawbacks of brush motors

(a) Generally noisy in use, especially at high spin speeds.
(b) Brush wear.
(c) Commutator wear/burning. Two or more segments linking together. This would cause sparking and overheating, resulting in poor running and eventual failure.
(d) Complete unit change needed if fault other than brushes. This is true of most makes except for Hoover, where most parts are available separately.

Main benefits of brush motors.

(a) In general, much cheaper than induction motors.
(b) Infinitely variable speed control available.
(c) Small in size.

Variations of brush motors

This type of G.E.C. motor can be found in many of today's automatic washing machines. Although similar models can be found in many different makes

and models of machine, they are not interchangeable, due to their different ratings of tacho coil and internal winding differences (for different speeds). When it is necessary to renew the motor, ensure that the new unit is *exactly* the same as the one to be replaced. To this end, always specify the make, model and serial number when purchasing a new unit.

This type of unit normally requires renewal if faulty, although some brushes and patterned armatures are available separately.

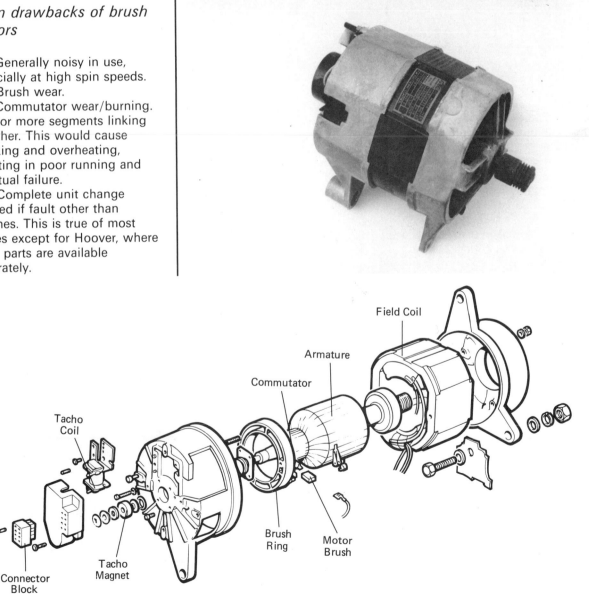

Field Coil

Armature

Commutator

Tacho Coil

Brush Ring

Motor Brush

Tacho Magnet

Connector Block

Shown is a typical Hoover motor. Many variations of this motor are currently available and are very similar. The motors look identical in every respect, except for the block connector at the rear. Although they look similar it is essential that you obtain the correct replacement unit for your machine. This motor is fully repairable and each component is available separately. Versions of this motor can be found on early Servis machines.

When obtaining replacement parts or replacement motors, ensure that you always give the make, model and serial number of your machine.

Armature change

The main aim of this photographic sequence is to show the removal of the motor from the machine, and the detailed removal and refitting of a new armature and brush ring. The motor shown is of a universal type to be found in many models of the Hoover range. It must be remembered that any connections that are to be removed should be noted to ensure their correct replacement at the end of the repair.

Also shown is the brush replacement for the G.E.C. type motor. Variations of which can be found in many machines such as Creda, Hotpoint and early Indesit. **Note:** Any other fault with this type of motor requires a complete change of unit as explained in the section: MAIN MOTORS.

Armature change – Hoover type model

1. Isolate the machine and remove the rear panel.

2. In this case a 'low insulation test' disclosed the motor fault. Remove the motor bolts and withdraw from the machine.

3. After noting the motor block colours, positions and connections, remove the plastic cover to reveal the tacho coil.

4. The tacho coil and magnet can be removed carefully. (The clip on the shaft can be lifted with a small screwdriver).

5. The four end rivets can be drilled out or removed with a sharp chisel, as in this instance.

6. Mark the position of the end frames, by marking with a pencil. When marked, remove the four securing bolts.

7. When the end bolts are removed, use a hide mallet (or similar) to free and remove the front end frame.

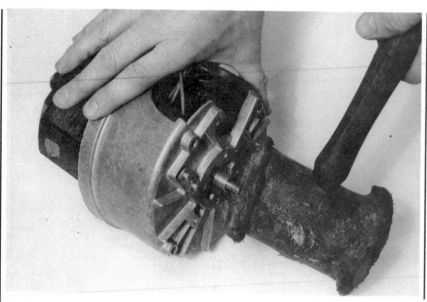

8. Knock the armature tacho end shaft free. Remove armature and inspect for faults. ◀

10. Check the bearings for free and quiet running by spinning them on the shaft. Also check for tight fit to shaft. (This one had damaged the shaft). ▼

9. Check copper segments on armature for damage, i.e., burnt looking or loose/raised segments, and for carbon build-up. (This one is badly damaged). ▲

11. New armature ready to fit. Note screw plates and screws instead of rivets to aid fitting. Fit replacement unit if in any doubt as to condition of old unit. ▶

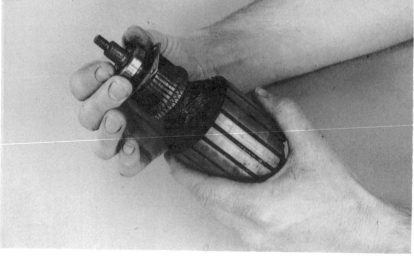

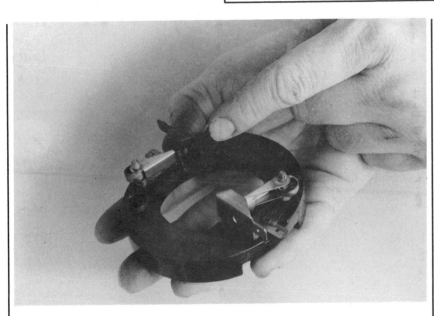

12. Old brush ring inspected for damage. Carefully check for smooth brush slides. Also check that no carbon deposits have caused low insulation. Change if in any doubt. (This one has burnt slides). ◄

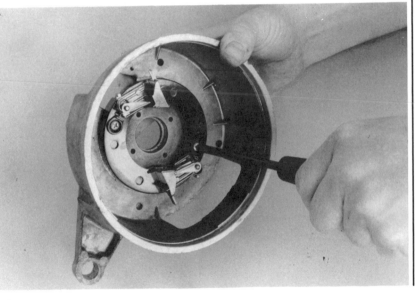

13. Fitting of new brush ring. If original unit cracked or damaged due to bad brushes, replace this unit. Slides should be smooth. ◄

15. New armature fitted to rear end frame. ▼

14. Shown are new and old brushes. The top lines show tagged and non-tagged type of brushes. The lower lines show split and worn brushes. ▲

16. Hold plate on inside of end frame with finger. Insert and tighten the securing screws.

17. Refit tacho magnet and clip. Ensure that when fitted the magnet will not turn on the shaft, i.e., it should be locked to the armature. ◀

18. Adjust tacho setting (if necessary). Screw centre up to the magnet and turn back 1^1/$_2$ turns only. ▼

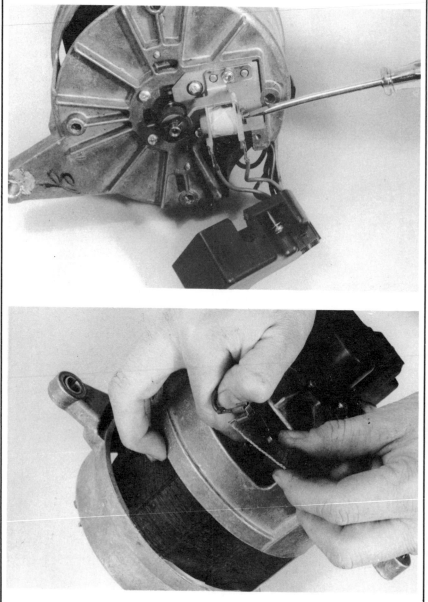

19. Refit front end frame and re-assemble motor, lining up the marks made in step 6. ▲

20. Fitting of new brushes. Ensure free movement of brush in slide. Make sure all connections are tight and do not foul metal body of motor. ◀

21. Ensure insulation strip is fitted to brush opening. It will fit easily if warmed first. The motor is now ready to fit to the machine for function testing when all panels have been refitted. ▲

GEC type motor (fault example)

1. GEC type motor. Early type can now have similar armature change as Hoover type, but generally only brushes fitted.

2. Removal of brush and holder from GEC type motor. Insert screwdriver and lift tongue of plastic at base of holder.

4. View of new brush and holder complete. Early screw-on type brush holders have separate brushes as above.

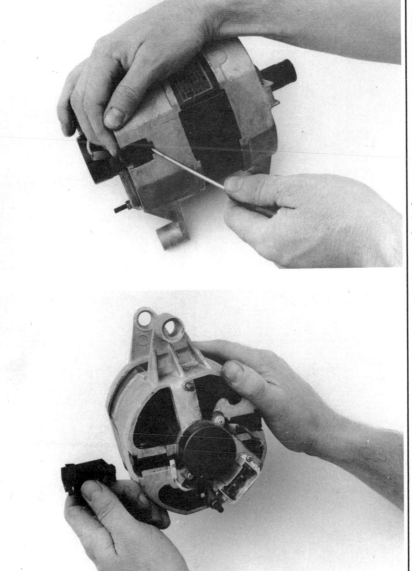

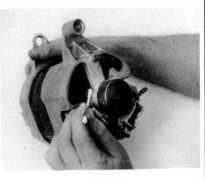

5. Ensure that any carbon dust deposits inside motor casing and armature are removed. (Blow out dust and clean with pipe cleaner or similar). Take care, do not inhale the dust.

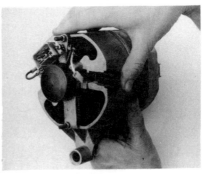

6. Refitting of GEC type brush holder and complete brush assembly. Slide back into position carefully ensuring that tongue of holder engages into position.

3. Slide out brush holder complete with brush. Note length of new brush and check for good movement of brush in slide. This brush has worn very short.

Indesit type motor (fault example)

1. View of Indesit type motor showing similarity to GEC type motor which was fitted to earlier Indesit washers. This motor replaces GEC versions.

2. Main differences are the length of mounting arms and style of brush gear. ▼

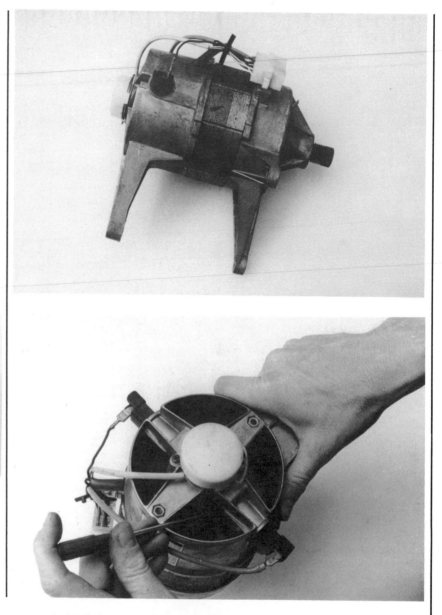

3. Brush holders are available as a spare part. Remove by pushing plastic locking tabs and pulling out holder. Pattern armatures can also be obtained for this style of motor. ▶

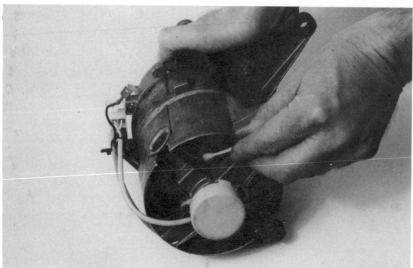

4. Ensure that any carbon dust deposits inside motor casing and armature are removed. (Blow out dust and clean with pipe cleaner or similar). Take care, do not inhale the dust. ◀

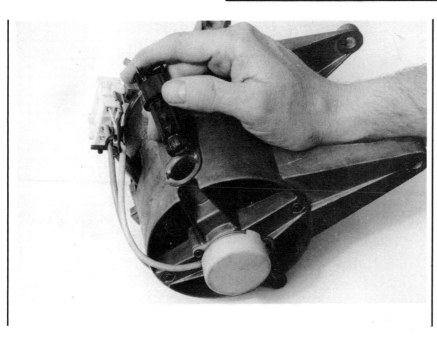

5. Cause of this motor fault was a sticking brush in the brush holder. New brush and holder cured the fault.

6. Refit new holder and complete brush assembly, taking care not to break or damage carbon brushes. ▲

Module control for brush motors

It must be remembered that all motor speed faults are not directly attributable to the motor. The fault could be caused by a piece of electronics called a module, that is connected between the timer and motor and controls the speed of the motor. There is no standard location for the module, but it is easily identified by its distinct printed circuit board (P.C.B.), and large heatsink.

How does it work?

The module obtains electrical information from both the timer and the motor. If the timer requires a wash speed it supplies power to the motor, whilst simultaneously switching in an appropriate resistor circuit in the module. There are two resistors in the example, therefore three speeds can be achieved, i.e., no resistors, one resistor, both resistors.

Wash speed – A, B and B, C closed: Therefore bypassing both resistors.

Distribute speed – A, B open, B, C closed: Therefore one resistor in circuit.

Spin speed – A, B and B, C open: Therefore both resistors are in circuit.

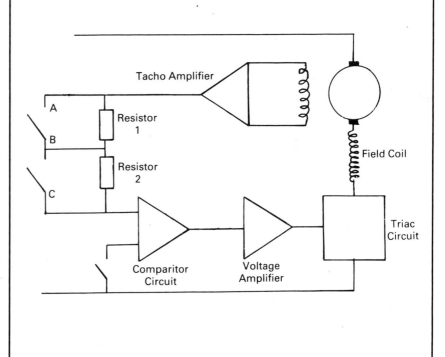

Washing Machine Manual

If the module interrupts the power supply to the motor at regular intervals it will in effect, pulse the motor. Pulsed at various speeds, it can be seen that the motor will slow down or speed up. On the rear end of the motor's armature is a circular magnet that revolves in unison with it. Near this magnet a coil of copper wire will be found. (Sometimes, this may be encased in plastic). This is called a tacho generator. If a magnet is rotated next to, or inside a coil of wire a current is produced. The current produced is proportional to the rotational speed of the magnet. In this case, the faster the motor is running the more current is produced. This current is fed to the module as a reference voltage. This is used to monitor the performance of the motor by comparing the relative speed of the motor with a known voltage via the comparitor circuit. If the reference voltage is found to be lower than the comparitor voltage, the module will increase the pulse rate, therefore increasing the speed of the motor. If the voltage is found to be high, the pulses are slowed, therefore decreasing the motor's speed. This happens many times a second, and is undetectable during normal operation. The diagram shown should help in understanding this principle.

How to check if the module is at fault.

If any of the internal components of the module have burned out, (i.e., charred or burnt looking), the motor should be checked for any shorting insulation or loose wires as these may be the probable cause.

Checks on the tacho magnet and tacho coil.

(a) If the magnet is loose or broken, this would result in incorrect speeds at lower motor speeds.
(b) Severe damage or complete loss of the magnet would cause the motor to spin on all positions.
(c) A break in the coil would result in a spin on all positions. A 'good' coil is usually about 200 to 1600 ohms resistance. If there is a break in the coil, the resistance is 0 ohms. The tacho generator is not returning any voltage therefore the module speeds the motor up. The increased speed is not transmitted back to the module, so the process is repeated *ad infinitum.*
(d) Breaks and/or poor connections of the wires leading to and from the tacho can have the same effect. This is especially true at the connection block with the motor, and the connection at the module.

Some modules fitted to modern machines have an inbuilt tacho test circuit, and will not operate if the tacho circuit is open.

It should be remembered that any loose connection will be aggravated by the movement of the tub on the suspension, and this should be taken into account when testing for such faults. The following chart can be used to help locate the module faults and show the correct course of action. Do not attempt to adjust the tacho other than as shown in the armature section.

The modules on the facing page are a small selection of modules that are fitted to today's automatic washing machines. Their appearance and function differ very little from one another, but are strictly *not* interchangeable. *Always ensure that the correct replacement unit is obtained. Always quote the make, model and serial number of your machine when ordering spare parts.*

If the fault persists the module is probably at fault. This should be replaced with a new unit, ensuring that the correct type is purchased. To fit, make a note of the connections, remove them and replace them on the new unit. It is important that the 'Duotine' connector fits tightly on the module. (The connections can be closed slightly by inserting a small screwdriver between the back of the TAG and the plastic duotine. Care should be taken not to close it too far as this may result in the tag not making contact.)

The machine must be isolated from the mains. Turn off at the wall socket and remove the plug.

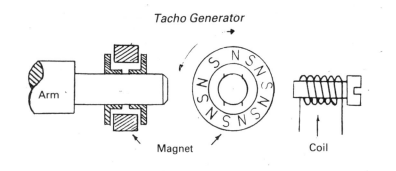

Tacho Generator

Arm

Magnet

Coil

Tacho generator

Warning: the machine must be isolated from the mains. Turn off at the wall socket and remove the plug.

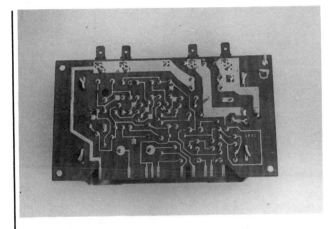

Hoover A/C.

Philips.

Creda A/C.

Hoover 1100.

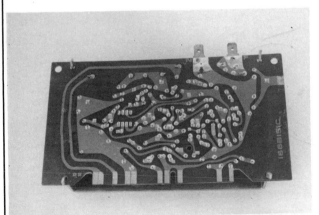

Servis A/C.

Hotpoint A/C.

Warning: The large metal back of the module is used as a heatsink. This means that it is *live* when in use, and therefore should be fitted correctly and securely to its plastic mounts. Even when testing, any contact with the earthed shell of the machine will render the unit useless.

Washing Machine Manual

Shown is the module from a Hotpoint Automatic. Note the discoloration that has occurred on the centre of the PCB (front). This is a sure sign that the module is at fault or will fault soon.

The reverse side of the PCB with the heat sink removed to show the components of the module clearly. The faulty components can be seen directly behind the area of discoloration. The component (a resistor in this case), has been overheating and subsequently failed. Repairs to modules are not merely a simple replacement of obvious components, as micro-chips within the circuit may have been damaged. We therefore advise that the module be removed and replaced with a complete new unit.

	Check Operation		Interlock	Motor	Tacho	Module		Tacho	Timer
			Check Interlock and Latch	Check Complete Motor Circuits	Check Circuit Late M/C's	Fit New One	Replace Original	Fit New One or Adjust	Check Timer moves on at all
Incorrect Drum Action	Spin	None	●	●	●	●			
		Slow		●	●	●			
		Cont		●		●			●
	Distribute	Cont	●	●	●	●			●
		None			●	●			
		Fast		●	●	●	●	●	
		Slow			●				
	Tumble	None	●	●	●	●			
		Fast			●	●	●	●	
		Slow		●	●	●	●	●	
		Cont							●

Induction motors

Induction motors (capacitor start)

Motors that can operate only on a/c mains, are called induction motors. They have no commutator or brushes, and the rotor is not directly connected to the mains supply. N.B. The rotor is the equivalent of the armature in brush motors. Although power is only fed to its stator coils, by an electrcal process called induction, the rotor also becomes magnetised.

When the current is switched on, it reverses the magnetic field in the stator coils 50 times per second. Magnetism is induced in the rotor. As a result of this, the stator attracts then repels the rotor at the same rate. Initial starting of an induction motor is by means of a start winding. This is a winding placed slightly out of synchronization with the other windings by means of a capacitor in its circuit. This imbalance causes rotation. This is a much simplified version of the true operation of an induction motor, as it is unnecessary to enter too deeply into its function at this stage.

Induction motors are simpler in design and construction than the brush type motor, and little maintenance is needed.

The new type of induction motor that is now gaining in popularity is of the type used by Fagor. This differs little from the normal induction motors and has windings for wash, spin and normal speeds. This also uses capacitor starting. It also has the addition of an external speed control module, a tacho coil and a magnet similar to that used in the brush type motors. This is described in greater detail later in this manual.

This module works on a similar basis to that used in the brush motor. (This is explained in the next section). In brief, it uses the tacho generator voltage to 'trip' the 'triac control' inside the module. This in turn modulates the main motor voltage by impulsing (increasing) the voltage by predetermined steps within the module circuit.

Simply, this means that speeds can be built up slowly and allows a slow build up to spin speed (unlike most motors where the speed selected is immediately engaged). This allows the clothes in the drum to balance out by centrifugal force, and results in much smoother spinning and less vibration of the machine. Another benefit of this is that a small potentiometer linked to the module and fitted to the facia panel of the machine could enable the user to vary the spin speed to their own desirable level (usually between 300-800 rpm, with a switch facility on the potentiometer for no spin at all).

Faults in either motor or module would require a complete change, as no internal components are available, except for the tacho coil.

Main drawbacks of induction motors. (Capacitor start)

(a) As all of the work is done by a complicated set of windings in the stator, this motor is generally not repairable and must be changed for a new unit.
(b) Capacitor failure often results in the motor failing to run. This often results in burn out, as the rest of the motor windings are receiving power, and no rotation is possible. Overheat is inevitable, even when TOC (Thermal Overload Cut-out) protected.

Main benefits of induction motors. (Capacitor start)

(a) Generally reliable.
(b) Quiet at all speeds.
(c) Can be run in both directions.

Main motor speed control (induction)

Induction motor speed control is achieved by the switching in and out of extra winding in the stator. This switching is done by the timer and no intermediary control is used other than one or two capacitors. For a detailed description of an induction motor, please refer to the section: MOTORS.

Warning: The machine must be isolated from the mains. Turn off at the wall socket and remove the plug.

The capacitor(s) will still contain a charge although the mains has been isolated. This must be discharged by using an electrically insulated screwdriver. Using this, 'short' the terminals of the capacitor with the shaft of the screwdriver ensuring that you are only in contact with the insulated handle.

It is not safe to proceed further until this has been done.

If the stator windings of an induction motor are faulty, it may continue to run, although it may appear sluggish and get extremely hot even when used for a short time. Therefore if you have been running the machine to determine the fault, proceed with care as the motor will remain hot for some time. If the motor appears to be very hot, the motor winding may be faulty and the unit should be replaced in a similar manner to that of the armature change.

Some induction motors may also be controlled by means of a module. Please refer to earlier section in the chapter regarding induction motors prior to suspecting a main motor fault with this type of machine.

Capacitor faults

A capacitor is a small device that stores electricity until a pre-determined level has been reached or it has been triggered. The stored energy is then released. The storage capacity of a capacitor is measured in microfarads (μF) and is displayed on the shell. Any replacement must be of the same μF rating.

If the motor fails to run on wash, but runs on spin and there are two capacitors fitted, it is possible that one of the capacitors is faulty. Change the capacitor with the lowest μF rating and re-test. In the case of one capacitor the motor should be checked. See section: MOTORS.

If the motor runs on wash, but fails on spin and there are two capacitors fitted, there are two possible faults. Change the capacitor with highest μF rating, and re-test. (Ensuring that the above warning is again noted). If the door interlock is connected directly to the motor spin circuit and the door is improperly closed this will stop the spin. As would a fault on the interlock itself. Please refer to the section: DOOR INTERLOCKS.

Typical capacitor for use with induction motors. Do not confuse capacitors with suppression units. They may look similar, but their functions differ.

Module as used for induction motor speed control. (Control voltage applied to the motor to give smoother operation and variable spin speeds.

Induction motors (Shaded pole)

The shaded pole motor is similar to the main induction motor in the respect that power is supplied to an outer winding only, and the rotor does not receive power. The major difference being the way that the initial rotation is induced. This is done by two copper segments that are bound around the iron segments of the stator. This causes a continuous imbalance in the magnetic field, therefore rotation.

Main drawbacks of induction motors (Shaded pole)

(a) Can be used in one direction only. This is governed by the positioning of the poles.
(b) Due to the permanent imbalance described on the previous page, this gives rise to excessive heat if used for long periods.
(c) Low starting power.
(d) If subjected to overheating for long periods, the motor will eventually fail – even if TOC protected.
(e) Generally not repairable.

Main benefits of induction motors (Shaded pole)

(a) Very cheap.
(b) Very reliable.
(c) Very quiet.
Note: TOC = Thermal Overload Cut-out.

This means that if the safe working temperature is exceeded, this device will sever the power supply to the motor. Most TOCs are now self-resetting, resulting in constant heating up and cooling down of the motor. If the fault is not spotted quickly, the TOC itself will fail, therefore causing motor failure.

Shown is the induction stator of a pump. The shaded poles are clearly visible by the two bands of copper inserted in opposing poles. Note the orientation of the copper bands before removing the stator from the pump. If the stator is re-fitted back to front, the pump will run in the opposite direction and not pump at all.

Shown here and over the page are a selection of induction motors that can be found on today's popular machines. Note that these are induction motors, and as such must be replaced as complete units. In most instances the only repairable items are the tacho coil and the pulley. Other individual components are not generally available.

Note: Although these motors may appear similar visibly, they are not interchangeable. It is advisable that you take the make, model and serial number of your machine to the supplier of your new motor, to ensure an exact replacement.

Large Bendix induction motor, giving 400/800 spin facility. Smaller versions can also be found on later machines. A new addition to this range is the module control induction motor, similar to the Fagor version (shown later).

This Zanussi motor is visibly similar to the Bendix motor, except for the round control block. This can also be found with a centrifugal pulley (as with the Candy, below).

This Candy motor has a centrifugal clutch/pulley system that increases the spin speed. (See foot of page).

Shown is a Fagor motor, typical of the new style induction motors, that are capable of variable speed build up via a module. Note the tacho connector at the rear of the motor.

Centrifugal pulleys

The centrifugal or variomatic pulley, is the large pulley that can be seen on some induction motors such as the Candy automatic.

What does it do?

It is fitted to help increase the drum speed when the machine spins.

How does it work?

Weights that are inside the pulley are 'pushed outwards' by centrifugal force when a fast motor speed is selected. As the pulley is constructed in two halves, the outward movement narrows the gap between the front and back plate of the pulley, therefore increasing its diameter.

This increase in diameter increases the 'drive ratio' between the drum pulley and the motor pulley. When the motor speed slows, the reverse occurs (i.e., the back plate moves away from the front plate) and the belt rides on the smaller diameter of the pulley. This can be seen in the photograph of the motor at rest.

Similar clutches can be found on Zanussi and Philips machines.

Candy machines also possess a similar centrifugal pulley on the drum, although this opens at the higher speeds, thus giving a smaller drive ratio.

This enables an increase in speed with a constant belt tension, without having to resort to expensive motor windings.

DO NOT overtighten the drive belt on machines with a centrifugal pulley.

Small Belt Drive Point

Centrifugal Weights

Fixed Pulley Front

Larger Belt Drive Point

Sliding Rear of Pulley

SLOW MOTOR SPEEDS

FAST MOTOR SPEEDS (SPIN)

OPERATION OF A CENTRIFUGAL PULLEY SYSTEM

Chapter 21.

Suppressors

The suppressor

In the module circuit there may be what appears to be a very large capacitor. This is in fact an 'in line suppressor'. Its function is to suppress (soak up) any interference caused by the machine, i.e., any sparking at the contact points of the commutator and brushes.

On later machines, this unit can be found connected directly in line with the mains supply entry point. There are at present three versions of this component currently in use. Occasionally short circuit problems may arise. This fault is easily identifiable by a possible splitting of the top section, and is often accompanied by a a burnt smell.

Identification between EARLY and LATE suppressors is quite easy. The new version is much smaller than the old, with the replacement of two 'spade' connectors for the 'flying lead' variety.

A revised version of suppression unit can be found in addition to those described above. This is an induction coil, fitted in series between the neutral position at the terminal block and the shell of the machine. As an induction coil is of far heavier gauge, it only passes suppression current, whereas the two earlier versions carry the full voltage load. Due to this, the temperature rise and associated problems are reduced in the new induction type. On some machines, a combination of both old and new types of suppressor can be found.

The two later versions require a good earth path of both plug and socket.

This unit should not be by-passed, as to have an unsuppressed machine is an offence because of the interference that it may cause to others.

Old style in line suppressor (variations possible).

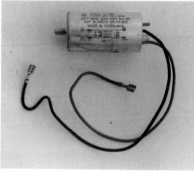

New style in line suppressor (variations possible).

Chapter 22.

Main bearing changes

Typical tapered bearing change

The following sequence of pictures shows the renewal of a set of drum bearings. In this machine, it was found that the main drum support bearings were worn and water damaged. This was caused by the carbon seal failing and allowing water and detergent to enter the bearing and housing.

This was suspected because of the noise of the machine, especially on spin and confirmed by removing the drive belt from the motor to the drum pulley, spinning the drum slightly by hand and listening for any grating noise. If this had been quiet, the motor would have been spun in the same way to test its bearings.

To confirm the drum bearing fault, another simpler method is to open the door of the machine and move the bottom of the door seal so as to see the inner drum and outer tub gap clearly, then try to lift the top lip of the drum only. At this point, the gap between the outer tub and inner drum should not increase nor decrease in size and no movement should be felt other than that of the outer tub on its suspension. This applies to all machines irrespective of bearing types. Picture 14 shows that the

drum and spider mount was breaking loose from its position on the drum, due to a form of metal fatigue fracturing the drum. The only possible cure for the fracture, was the fitting of a complete new drum assembly. The initial fault was also rectified, being a renewal of the bearings. (The user was unfortunate in needing the drum unit, especially when the support shaft itself was in such good condition).

The removal of the drum and back half assembly on this style of machine is quite straightforward, and this style of drum and back half are fitted to many of the leading makes (including Hoover, Hotpoint, Creda and late Servis) although in each case the size of bearing and type of carbon seal differ slightly between machines. As the bearing kits are complete matched sets, no problems should arise.

After isolating the machine and laying it face down on a suitable surface, the removal of the back panel will reveal the back half and outer securing nuts. All of the nuts and bolts securing the back half and tub should be removed. (If necessary the top of the machine may be

removed to gain access to the top bolts.)

When this is done, mark all of the connections to the heater and thermostat and disconnect them. The back half assembly can now be manoeuvred from its position and removed from the back of the machine. (The back half is made watertight by a rubber seal around itself and the tub. If the back half sticks to the tub, and all of the necessary nuts and bolts have been removed, gently prise the back half from the tub ensuring that no excessive force is used.)

The removal of the pulley and bearings can now proceed.

If the bearing set for your machine is of the ordinary ball bearing type, the job is much easier as the old bearing should knock out in one piece. Should this type of bearing 'collapse' or leave its outer shell, the shell can be removed as shown for the taper bearing shell in picture 18. Care must be taken not to go too deep with the drill into the soft aluminium housing.

When greasing the new bearing, (this is obviously not necessary on the sealed bearing type) take care not to over-grease them, as this will not help lubricate it and in fact will considerably reduce the bearing life.

The new taper bearing kit will come complete with an odd shaped aluminium washer that fits between the rear bearing spacer and pulley. This is known as a torque washer and is essential for the correct operation of the bearing. Always fit a new torque washer to this type of bearing if the pulley is removed for any reason. The torque washer is a simple way of putting the taper bearings under a known pressure without the use of a torque wrench.

When fitted together, the torque washer collapses at a given pressure and dispenses with the need for a torque wrench for tightening the pulley bolt.

A full set of instructions for the torque washer will come with the new bearing kit, however we have included a typical bearing change below.

If your machine is of the type with ball bearings, please disregard the paragraph concerning torque washers, as this type of bearing assembly does not require a torque setting. Renewal of this type of bearing is a simple reversal of the strip-down procedure.

Instructions for bearing change

1. How to dismantle the old pulley and bearings.

(i) Remove the bolt (1) and washers (2 and 3) securing the tub pulley and remove the pulley (4).
(ii) When removing the tub gasket, check for any wearing. It is advisable to replace this item to ensure a true seal between the inner drum and outer tub.

2. Extraction of old bearings.

(i) The existing bearing sleeves (9 and 11) will be found inside the tub backplate (10). Extract the bearing sub assemblies and then apply heat to the area containing the sleeves. The sleeves can then be gently tapped out with a small chisel, drift or screwdriver.

3. Renewal of bearings.

(i) Push the new sleeves into place, ensuring that the inner surface of the tub backplate is thoroughly cleaned.
(ii) Insert the first (larger) bearing and washer (12).
(iii) Gently push the seal (13) into place. It is advisable to use a waterproof adhesive around the seal to prevent leaking.
(iv) Clean the new carbon face seal thoroughly to remove all traces of grease, oil, etc. Replace the spacer washer over the seal.
(vi) It is advisable to fit new washers to the front and rear (12 and 7) as it is likely they have been scoured by the faulty bearings. (Many bearing kits do not contain items 12 and 7 and these may have to be obtained separately.

4. Inserting the torque washer.

(i) Re-assemble the remaining parts in reverse order to that in which they were removed. Do not use the old torque washer (6) – Only use the new washer supplied with the kit.
(ii) Fit the shim washer from the kit under the torque washer. (In the position shown in (6A)).
(iii) Tighten the bolt (1) against the pulley as far as possible without locking the tab washer.
(iv) Complete the tightening operation until the 'D' washer fits firmly against the shoulder of the spider unit. (5).
(v) The spacer is now pre-set. It is essential to do this, in order to ensure the correct loading pressure on the bearings.

5. Discard shim and complete re-assembly.

(i) Remove the bolt (1), washers (2 and 3), pulley (4) and spacer (6). Discard the shim (6A).
(iii) Re-assemble in reverse order again. This time locking the tab washer against the bolt.

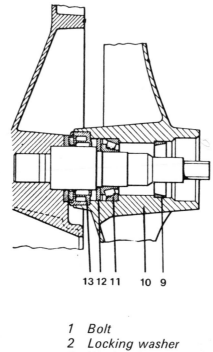

13 12 11   10 9   8   7 6 6a 5   4   3 2   1

1	Bolt	7	Washer (thin)
2	Locking washer	8	Small bearings
3	Washer (small)	9	Bearing sleeve
4	Pulley	10	Tub backplate
5	'D' washer	11	Bearing sleeve
6	Spacer	12	Washer (thick)
6a	Shim (disposable)	13	Carbon face seal

(iii) Failure to follow this procedure on taper roller bearings will result in shortening the life of the new bearing set considerably.

Below are a few helpful hints on the refitting of the assembly back in the machine.

(a) It is advisable to remove the heater from the back half before refitting the back half and drum into the machine. Refitting the heater in this fashion ensures the correct location of the internal heater securing clip.

(b) A thermostat pod (if applicable) and the heater grommet can be helped by a smear of sealant to help slide them into position. If the thermostat grommet looks perished, this should be changed.

(c) Remember to reseal any hoses on the pressure system if they have been disturbed.

(d) Always remember to fit a new tub back half seal.

(e) Check the tension on the main drive belt and adjust the belt if necessary. This is done by moving the motor up or down to slacken or tighten the belt. (Like adjusting a fan belt on a motor car.) Do not overtighten the belt.

Main drum bearing repair (Hoover)

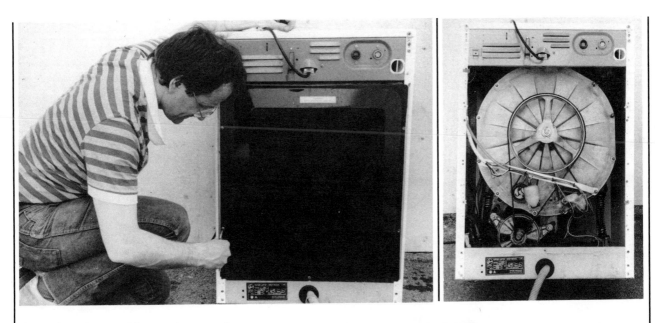

1. Isolate the machine and remove the rear panel. Note all connections to the back plate. ▲

Above right:
2. Protect the face of the machine and gently lay the machine on its front.

3. Note the position and angle of pressure vessel and remove. ▶

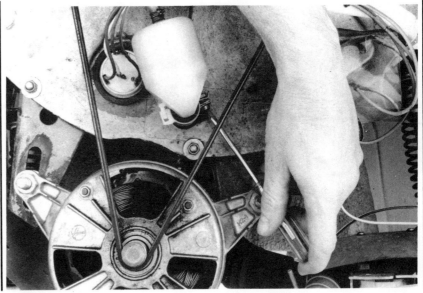

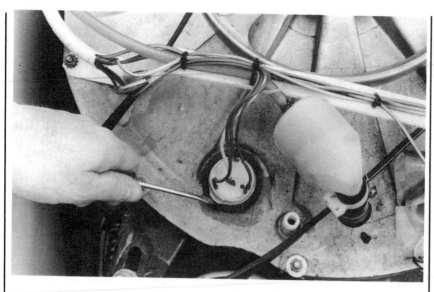

4. Note connections on the thermostat. Remove thermostat with the wires still connected. Use a flat bladed screwdriver to ease it from the seal. ◄

5. Having noted the wiring connections, they can now be removed. Slacken the heater clamp nut and gently prise the heater free. ▶

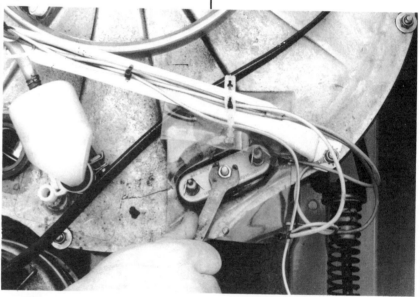

6. Remove back half bolts from around the perimeter of the tub.

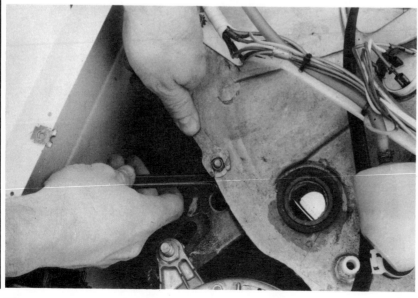

7. The discharge from the drain hole can be seen here, and indicates water penetration of the bearings. The discharge is a mixture of grease, rust and water.

8. With all fixing bolts removed and wires secured out of the way, the drum and back half can be manoeuvred free from the tub.

9. With drum and bearing unit completely removed from the machine it is much easier to work on. ◄

11. Remove the pulley bolt, pulley and spacers, etc., noting their correct order. ▲

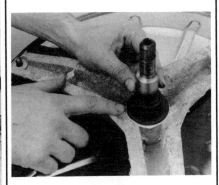

10. Unlock the tab on the pulley bolt with the aid of a flat bladed screwdriver.

12. Backplate freed from the drum shaft. (The front bearing may seize on the shaft and will have to be drawn off with pullers. If this happens, protect the shaft end by re-fitting the bolt onto the end of the shaft. This protects the shaft and aids the location of the puller centre).

13. Check shaft carefully for wear and ridges at the bearing support points. (Front and rear). Also check carbon face for cracks or loose fit. The example shown is OK.

14. (see photo 12) Check the three mounting points for cracks etc. This drum and shaft are crush bolt fitted, therefore any fault on the drum or shaft requires a complete drum. Not all machines have this system.

15. Insert screwdriver and prise out bearing carbon face seal.

16. Remove old washer and front bearings. In this case a taper bearing was found. Ball bearings will have to be knocked out with a metal drift.

17. With rear bearing removed, knock out rear bearing shell/liner by the inner lip.

18. If there is no visible lip to the front bearing shell, drill two slots opposing each other in the inner of the housing to expose the liner. Do not drill too deeply.

19. Position of drill mark on front inner.

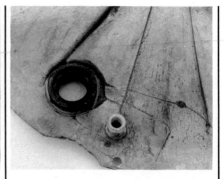

20. Remove the old thermostat seal if it is found to be a poor fit, or perished. Apply sealant to the new seal to ensure a good watertight seal.

21. Clean all seal and bearing surfaces prior to refitting new parts.

22. New set of taper roller bearings, torque washer and carbon seal suitable for this machine.

Centre photo:
25. Now insert front liner and repeat operation as in step 24.

26. Grease bearings back and front and re-assemble as described in text.

23. Typical set of ball bearings. Seals and bearing sizes may differ. Not interchangeable with taper bearings, not suitable for this machine.

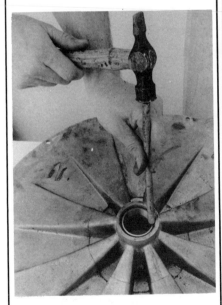

27. Back half ready to be fitted to the drum shaft.

24. Insert rear bearing liner and tap into position firmly, seating to its base using a soft metal drift.

28. Following the instructions for use of torque washer and shim, the unit is made ready for fitting back into the machine. Make sure that you reset the lock tab on the pulley bolt. ▶

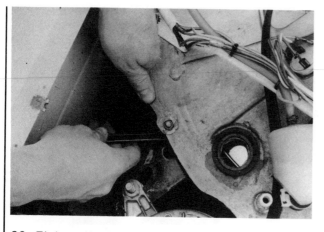

29. Tighten the bolts in sequence slowly using opposing bolts. Do not overtighten.

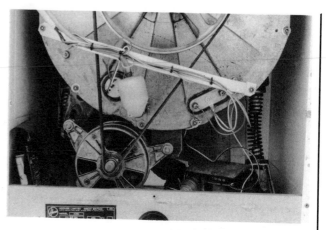

30. Seal and refit all hoses and grommets and secure all connections to the heater, etc. Adjust the belt tension prior to the functional test with all panels in position.

Hotpoint drum bearing removal

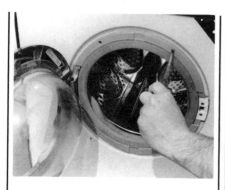

1. With machine isolated, open door and remove the securing screws for the plastic surround for the door seal.

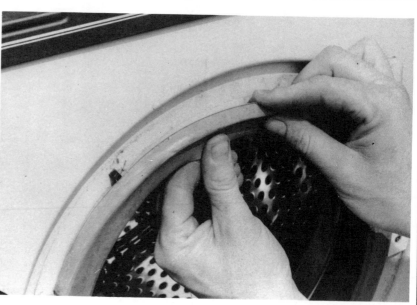

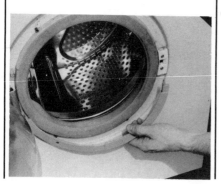

2. Next, remove the door seal surround carefully. This is in two halves (top and bottom).

3. Free the door seal from the outer shell lip of the machine and allow to rest on inside of the front panel.

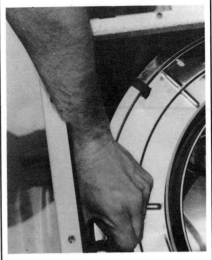

4. Remove the screws holding the timer knob in position. On early models, only one plastic screw will be found. ◄

9. Note the position of the clips securing the front of the outer tub and remove carefully. ▲

5. Pull to remove the soap drawer and remove the exposed screws. This allows the front facia to be removed.

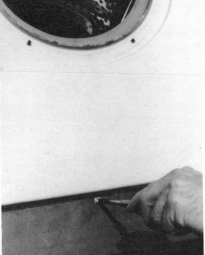

7. Remove the screws securing the bottom of the front panel. Hexagonal headed bolts may be found on early models. ◄

8. With front panel off, remove the door catch and interlock (if fitted). ▼

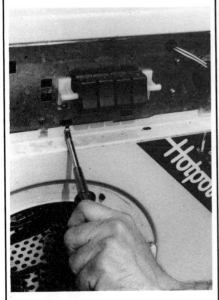

6. Remove the screws securing the top of the front panel. ▲

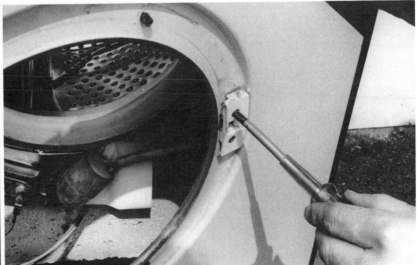

10. With the clips removed, the tub front can be removed completely. Take care not to damage heater or connections.

11. Remove the screws securing the rear panel to expose the drum pulley.

12. Remove the pulley lock nut (right hand thread) and 'chock' the pulley against the tub with a wedge of wood. ▼

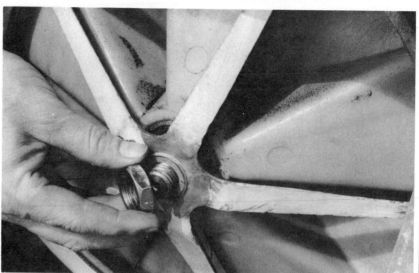

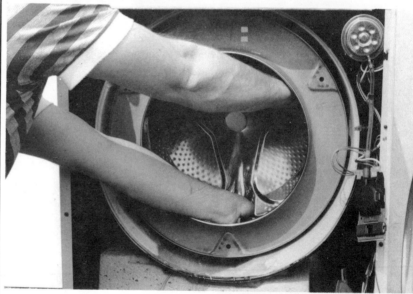

13. With the pulley securely wedged, grasp inner paddles of the drum and turn anti-clockwise. This will unscrew the pulley. ▲

14. With pulley removed, tap the drum shaft free from the bearings using a soft-headed mallet.

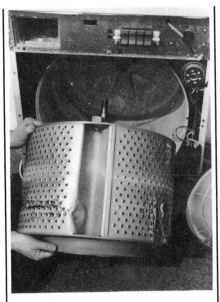

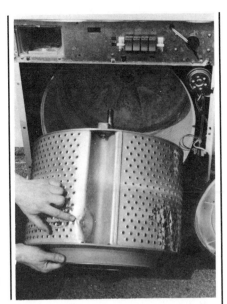

15. Withdraw the drum and shaft from the tub. This will allow ample room to 'drift' out the ball bearings and shaft seal. Bearing replacement for this type of drum is quite straight-forward. using a soft drift, knock the new bearing home, taking care not to damage the new seal. Re-assembly of your machine is a reversal of the previous procedure.

16. This machine also had severe drum damage as indicated.

17. This style of machine has a 'catch pot' style filter in the sump hose. When removed a large amount of coins, metal screws, curtain hooks and various other household items were found.

18. These items should not have been allowed to enter the machine. They have damaged the drum severaly. What would have been a relatively inexpensive 'bearing only' repair, has now required the renewal of a costly drum. (The £1.44 that was found did not cover the cost of the new drum!). This could have been avoided with a little care and attention to pockets, etc., when loading the machine.

Bearing changes needing tub removal

On several makes of machine, especially those with friction damper and top support spring suspension, to make any repair to the drum bearings, tub seals, outer or inner drum renewal it will be necessary for the outer and inner drum unit to be removed from the shell of the machine.

In general, the removal of this large unit is via the top of the machine shell. The following text describes the removal of the outer tub after removing such items as the top tub weights, pulley, all connections and hoses to the unit. A photo sequence is not used for this as it would tend to mislead rather than help.

Once removed, the unit is easily accessible and the bearing renewal is similar to that shown in the photo sequence.

Indesit, Zanussi and late Bendix automatics are the exception to this rule, where, although friction dampers are used, the bearings can be changed without removing the outer tub. In the case of the Indesit machine a bearing change is easier if the complete drum spider and bearing unit is fitted, as this is separate from the drum, itself. The Zanussi and late Bendix bearings are housed in an external housing that can be removed from the outer tub via the rear opening.

The servicing of many types of drum, bearing, outer tub and seals will entail the removal of the outer tub from the machine. This is done by withdrawing the outer tub from the top of the machine's cabinet as a complete unit. It is advisable to remove all knobs from the front of the machine, to reveal the fixing screws of the item behind the knob. These should be unscrewed and laid over the front facia of the machine. Do not disconnect any wiring.

Release the screws securing the dispenser unit to the cabinet and remove the dispenser hose from the dispenser unit. Lay the dispenser unit over the front of the machine. Remove the top tub weight (if fitted), and release the front fitting of the door seal.

To help slide the tub unit out of the machine, two pieces of wood (2" x 1" x 4') can be inserted down the left hand side of the machine between the tub and cabinet to support the tub during its removal (See diagram 1). **Note:** If your machine has the timer on the opposite side to that shown in diagram 1, the wood should be inserted down the right hand side and the machine laid over correspondingly.

Now lower the machine onto the left hand side, making sure that the cabinet side and floor are protected, and release the shock absorber or friction damper mountings. Now disconnect the sump hose, pressure hoses, heater connections, thermostat connections and motor block connections. Remove drive belt and drum pulley, and check that all connections are free from the outer tub unit. At the top of the machine, release the suspension springs by pushing the tub unit towards the top of the machine.

It will now be possible to slide the tub assembly out of the cabinet. (At this point, a little help may be useful as the unit will be quite heavy and needs manoeuvring out of position). At this time ensure that the lower friction bracket is being supported by one of the wooden strips. It is wise to hold the door open during the tub withdrawal.

After making note of all clamp positions, tub front and back positions, the repair can now be carried out.

It is wise to re-seal and check all hoses and their fixing points prior to refitting the unit. It is important to do this when the tub is out of the machine, as it would be very difficult when the unit is replaced.

Refitting is a reversal of the removal procedure. After refitting, ensure that a test sequence is operated.

Note: There are some machines on the market with detachable front panels. Two of these are Fagor and Hotpoint. The latter being the version with the plastic/nylon outer tub fitted. With this type of machine, the drum and bearing assemblies can be removed and changed with the other tub *in situ*, thus avoiding the extra work involved in tub removal.

With the Hotpoint machine, the pulley is threaded to the shaft, and is secured by a locknut. To release the pulley, chock it with wood and rotate the drum anti-clockwsie from the front of the machine. When refitting, apply some locking compound to the shaft thread. (This can be obtained from any good D.I.Y. or motorists shop).

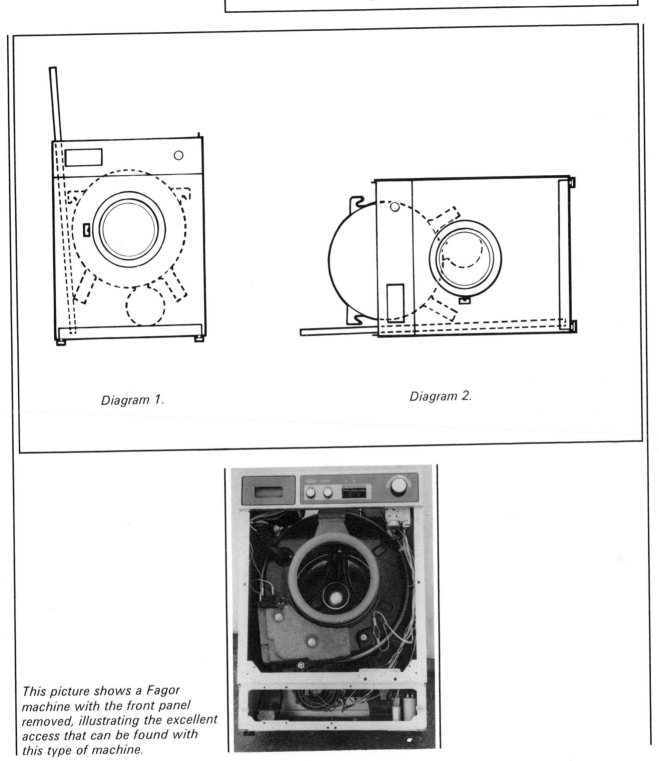

Diagram 1.

Diagram 2.

This picture shows a Fagor machine with the front panel removed, illustrating the excellent access that can be found with this type of machine.

Chapter 23.

Electrical fault finding

Electrical fault finding (using a meter)

Setting it up

In this book, the term 'meter' is used to describe a multimeter. This is a meter to test continuity, i.e., to see if a circuit is an 'open circuit' (to allow no current through), or 'closed circuit' (to allow current through).

There are several types of meters available today, and all are much the same with only minor external differences. Some may have a rotary selector switch that changes the function of the meter and two holes where the small testing wires are attached, and some may have several labelled 'holes' where the testing wires attach.

The first meter described is the most straightforward to use. Set the selector switch to ohms (Ω) and place the testing wires in the correct holes. These are positive (+ve) for red and negative (−ve comm) for black. With the second meter, the function of the meter changes depending where the testing wires are attached. To test for continuity, the positive (red) wire must be placed in the hole marked Ω, and the negative (black) must be placed in the

negative common D.C. or D.C. comm Ω. If the meter only has a negative hole, this will be acceptable for the negative (black) wire.

To test if the meter is now working, ensure that the test wires are properly attached, and the selector switch (if any) is selected to ohms (Ω). Look at the dial on the meter, and the needle should be resting on its stop at one end of the dial on or past the 100 ohms mark. Now press the two ends of the wires together and the needle should swing towards the 0 ohms mark and stay there. This then shows that there is no broken circuit, i.e., continuity.

An alternative to a meter

If you have not got a meter and still need a continuity test, it is very easy to build a device that will do the same job for a fraction of the cost.

Using the suspected lack of continuity to its full advantage, we can test for this using a standard battery, bulb and three wires (1 x 5", and 2 x 10"). Connect the small wire to the positive (+ve) terminal of the

battery and the other end of that wire to the centre terminal of a small torch bulb that works. Attach one of the other wires to the negative terminal of the battery and leave the other end free. The other wire should be attached to the negative (−ve or body) of the bulb and again, leave the end free.

The two loose wires now act as the test wires on the meter. Press the two ends of the wire together, and the bulb should light. If not check that the battery has power, and that the bulb is OK. This now is the same as the meter. When 'open circuit', the light will stay off, and when 'closed circuit' the light will turn on.

Ensure that the machine is isolated from the main supply before attempting to use a meter.

How to test for continuity

To test for an open circuit, note and remove the original wiring to the component to be tested. (If this is not done, false readings may be given from other items that may be in circuit). The ends of the two wires (on either the meter or the bulb,) should be

attached to the component that is
suspected. For example, to test a
heater for continuity, place the
meter wires on the tags at the
end of the heater and watch the
meter or bulb. The bulb should
light and/or the needle should
swing towards zero. (At this
stage, it does not matter if the
needle does not reach zero or if
the bulb is not very bright.)

If the heater is open circuit ,
i.e., no movement or light, the
heater can then be suspected and
tested further. If closed circuit,
the heater is OK.

For your convenience, the
correct states of several
components are listed below.

*A multimeter of the type to be
found in most D.I.Y. stores. Try to
obtain a meter with a good
informative booklet. The meter
shown was purchased for under
£10.00 and proved to be useful
for many other jobs around the
house and car.*

The one hundred ohms referred
to, is not the ohms rating of the
item, but the maximum the meter
in use could read. As this ohms
reading will differ from item to
item, this test is for open or
closed circuit tests only. Any
reference to an ohms ( ) reading
is a guide only, as resistances
differ on components from
machine to machine. The
objective is to test for either
continuity or the lack of
continuity of the item.

Component	State	Typical resistances found	Special notes
Plug fuse	Light on		Check correct rating and condition of plug, fuse and socket. Change if found to be defective in any way.
Inlet valves	Light on	10,000 Ω	If the circuit is OK, possible manual fault inside valve.
Heater	Light on	22 Ω	Check also for low insulation.
Pressure switch	Both encountered		See PRESSURE SWITCH section.
Thermostat	Both encountered		See THERMOSTAT section.
Outlet pump	Light on	45 Ω	If the circuit is OK, possible manual fault inside pump.
Main motor	Light on		Refer to MOTOR section for help and check motor brushes (if any).
Tacho coil (if fitted)	Light on	200 Ω up to 1600 Ω	Refer to MOTOR section
Harness wiring	Light on		Test each wire separately to suspect component pulling connections along its length to find possible internal open circuit, although outer insulation may appear complete.

2. The testing of this water valve proved that the coil was open circuit. This is shown by the meter needle staying at its 'rest' position. This shows that the 'no fill' fault on the machine was in fact due to the water valve failing to energise and allow water into the machine. (On components such as these, it is a good idea to try to move the terminals as a poor internal connection may cause the bad reading). This problem was cured by renewing the valve.

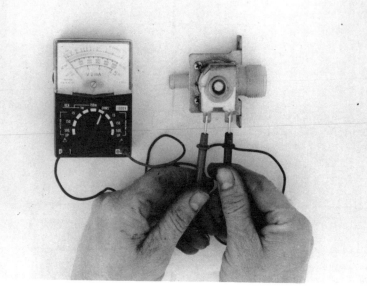

1. The testing of the heater element to check for a circuit 'through' it. In this instance, the heater does have a circuit as shown by the meter needle at 100. This means that the 'no heat' fault on the machine is not a fault of this component. The next step would be to test the wiring and connections to and from the heater in the same way. Also check the timer and/or the thermostat if in the heater circuit.

Chapter 24.

Wiring harness faults

Wiring harness faults

What is a wiring harness?

The term harness is used for all of the wires that connect the various components within the machine. They are usually bound or fastened together in bunches to keep the wiring in the machine neat and safely anchored.

What does it do?

At first sight, the harness may look like a jumble of wires thrown together. This is not the case. If you take the time to inspect the harness, you will find that each wire is colour coded or numbered (either on the wire itself, or on the connector at either end). This allows the engineer to follow the wire through the machine easily. With practise, any wiring codings can be followed.

As most of the wires in the machine either finish or start at the timer unit, it may be helpful to think of the timer as the base of a tree, with the main wiring harness as the trunk. As the trunk is followed, branches appear (i.e., wires to the valves, pressure switches, etc.). As the trunk continues upwards, it slowly gets thinner and branching takes place to the motor, pump, module, etc.

Each item is therefore separate, but linked to the timer by a central bond of wire. This can be likened to a central command post, communicating with field outposts,

The connecting wires to and/or from a component are vital to that component and possibly others that rely on that items' correct functioning.

Luckily wiring faults are not too common. When these faults do occur, they usually seem to result in big problems, when in truth only a small fault has occurred, i.e., one poor connection can cause a motor not to function at all, and render the machine unusable.

Do not fall into the trap of always suspecting the worst. Many people including engineers, blindly fit parts such as a motor or a module for a similar fault to that mentioned, only to find it did not cure the problem. Unfortunately the timer is usually blamed and subsequently changed. This does not cure the problem and is an expensive mistake.

Stop, think and check all wires and connections that relate to your particular fault.

Always inspect all connections and ensure that the wire and connector has a tight fit. Loose or poor connections can overheat and cause a lot of trouble, especially on items such as the heater.

Poor connections to items such as the main motor or pump will be aggravated by the movement of the machine when in use and may not be so apparent when the test is carried out.

One of the most difficult faults to find is where the metal core of the wire has broken and the outer insulation has not. This wire will appear perfect from the outside but will pass no electrical current. To test for this, see the section: USING A METER.

It must be remembered that such faults may be intermittent. That is to say that one reading may be correct, and the same test later may prove incorrect. This is due to the movement of the outer insulation of the wire first making, then breaking the electrical connection.

When testing for such intermittent faults, it is wise to

pull or stretch each wire tested, as an unbroken wire will not stretch. A wire that is broken will stretch at the break point and rectification is a simple matter of renewing the connection with a suitable connector.

Do not make the connection by twisting the wires together and covering them with insulation tape – remember a fifteen pence connector is much cheaper than a new motor you did not really need. Take time to do a few simple checks – it saves time, patience and money.

Note: Please ensure that the harness is secured adequately to the shell of the machine, but also ensuring free movement to such items as the motor, heater, etc.

Take care that any metal fastening clips do not chafe the plastic insulation around the wires. Also ensure that the wires are not in contact with sharp metal edges such as self tapping screws.

Please note: Before attempting to remove or repair the wiring harness or any other component in the machine, isolate the machine from the main electrical supply by removing the plug from the wall socket.

Various harness connections

Male Terminal   Female Terminal

Harness connection. Can often be of a multi block fitting of several wires in one moulded block.

Female spade terminal.

In line connector used for low amperage.

Insulation cover.

Butt connector for connecting several wires together.

Large in line connector used for high amperage wires.

Piggy back terminal for two wires to one terminal.

All of the above are 'crimp' fitted to inner and outer of the wires. When used make sure that they fit securely and will not easily part.

The terminal block is the first distribution point of the power into the machine. Ensure all connections are sound, as heat will be generated if not.

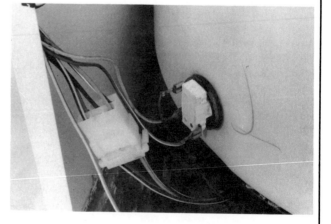

Harness connector block. Again any loose connectors will overheat and cause problems. Ensure a secure fit.

Chapter 25.

Useful tips and information

Useful tips and information

1. Shown above in the centre are the various types of clips in common use in today's machines. In the centre are the screw type wire clips. Top right is the new type toothed clip. This new clip is much easier and quicker to fit as grips or pliers are used to tighten jaws together. Left are two types of corbin spring clips. Care should be taken in removing this type of clip, as they have a tendency to 'spring' – even under tension. For removal, corbin pliers are best, however, with care, ordinary grips may be used. Lower right is a worm drive or jubilee clip. This again is a simple but effective clip.

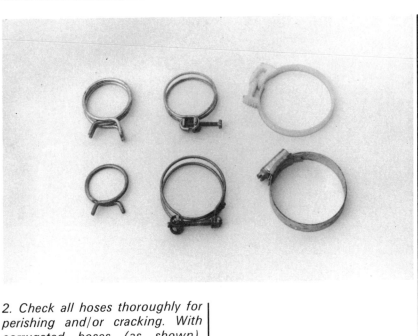

2. Check all hoses thoroughly for perishing and/or cracking. With corrugated hoses (as shown), stretch the hose to ensure a thorough check. (It is wise to check any new hose before fitting). ◀

3. On some machines the door interlock jams the door shut when it fails. As the fixing screws are behind the locked door, it may be difficult to open the door. It is possible to move the door latch with a screwdriver, as shown. Be careful not to scratch the paintwork. ▶

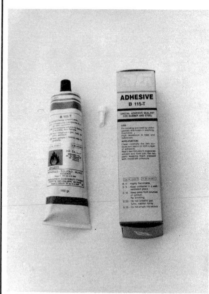

4. A little washing-up liquid or fabric conditioner can be smeared on grommets or rubber mouldings.

5. Sealants like the one shown can be used for pressure system hoses and for aiding the fitting and sealing of new hoses, grommets, etc. ▲

6. Some machines may have a wire surrounding the door seal. This retaining ring can be removed using a flat bladed screwdriver. The machine shown is a Fagor. ▲

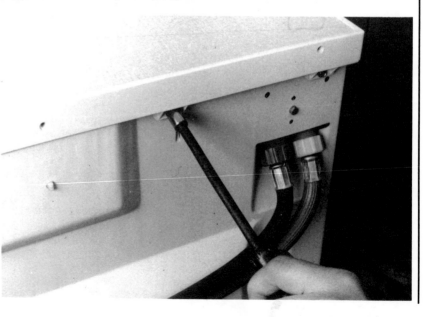

7. On some machines with fitted worktops, the top removal is not as straightforward. Firstly, remove the self-tapping bolts on the rear plastic panel section. ▶

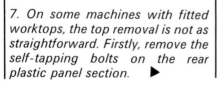

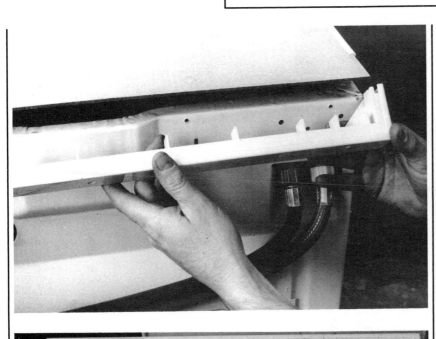

8. Remove the rear plastic surround completely. As always, ensure that the machine is isolated. This is because many machines will reveal open terminals behind the plastic moulding. ◄

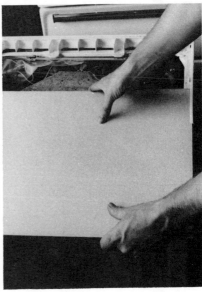

9. The top is now ready to be moved from its position. Push or pull the top towards the back of the machine and remove. This may require some force, especially if the top has not been removed for some time. ▲

10. Access to the top half of the machine is now possible. To aid the refitting of the top, a little washing-up liquid may be smeared on the plastic slides of the machine. ▲

11. Rear access to this type of machine is limited to a much smaller rear opening. Any repairs to this type of machine will require the inner and outer tub assembly to be removed via the top of the machine. Please refer to the section on BEARINGS. ▶

Chapter 26.

Buying spare parts

Buying spare parts

The aim of this manual has been to assist in the D.I.Y. repair of your automatic washing machine. We hope that you will now not only possess a greater knowledge of how your machine works, but also the knowledge to prevent faults.

Above all, we hope that, armed with this information, you will feel confident enough to tackle most (if not all) of the faults that may arise with your machine from time to time.

All of this knowledge and new-found confidence would however, be wasted if you could not locate the parts that you require to complete the repair.

In the past this would have been somewhat of a problem, but in recent years the availability of spares has increased. This is for several reasons.

1. The reluctance of people to pay high call-out and labour charges for jobs that they feel they can do themselves.
2. The general interest in household D.I.Y. coupled with the saving from call-out and labour charges, gives a feeling of satisfaction when the job is finally complete.
3. The growth in size and number of D.I.Y. stores in recent years.

4. The improvement in the availability of pre-packed spares.

Many independent domestic appliance companies have been reluctant to supply parts for the D.I.Y. market in the past, but the current trend is to expand the amount of pre-packed spares for the public. This has been confirmed by the three biggest independent spares suppliers of genuine and non-genuine (patterned) spares. The range of 'off the shelf' spare parts in both retail outlets and mail order companies is most welcome, and many machine manufacturers, who do not have local dealerships, will supply parts by post if requested. (Unfortunately this can sometimes be a lengthy process).

By far the best approach to obtaining the parts you require is to find a local 'spares and repairs' dealer through the Yellow Pages or local press. This is best done before your machine breaks down as you will then not waste time when a fault arises. In many instances you may possess more knowledge of your machine than the assistant in the shop, so it is essential to take the make, model and serial number of your machine with you to help them locate or

order the correct spare part for your needs.

You may also find it quite advantageous to take the faulty part(s) with you whenever possible, to confirm visually that it is the correct replacement, i.e., most pumps will look the same from memory, although quite substantial differences may be seen if the faulty item is compared with the newly offered item. The casing or mounting plate, etc., may be different.

It is most annoying to get home from the repair shop only to find that two extra bolts are required.

Patterned parts

Certain parts that are widely available are marked 'suitable for' or 'to fit'. These are generally called 'patterned', 'patent' or 'bojack' parts. Such terms refer to items or parts that are not supplied by the manufacturer of your machine, but are designed to fit it.

Some are copies of genuine parts and others are supplied by the original parts manufacturer to an independent distributor which are then supplied to the retailer and sold to the customer. This avoids the original manufacturer's mark-up as it is not an 'official' or 'genuine' spare part. This saving is then passed on to the customer.

Many of the washing machine manufacturers disliked this procedure in the past, as the parts were of an inferior quality.

This however, is not the case today as the supply of parts is very big business and quality has improved dramatically. Although great savings can be made, care must be taken not to save money by buying inferior spare parts. Check the quality of the item first wherever possible.

A reputable dealer should supply only good quality patterned or genuine parts

Many of the original machine manufacturers are now discounting their genuine authorised spares to combat the growth in patterned spares. This is very good, as it can only benefit you, the consumer.

Genuine parts

Parts supplied by the manufacturer of your machine or by their authorised local agent, are classed as "genuine" and will in many cases, carry the company's trade mark or colours, etc. Many of the parts in today's machines are in fact not produced by the manufacturer of the finished machine, but a sub-contractor who also may supply a distributor of patterned spares with identical items.

Patterned spares producers will only take on items that have volume sales and leave the slow moving items to the original manufacturer of the machine. It is this that angers the manufacturer. Generally it is a long procedure to obtain spares 'direct' from the manufacturer as many are unwilling to supply small orders direct to the public. Another system used to deter small orders is to use a 'pro-forma' invoicing sheet that will delay the receipt of parts until your cheque has

cleared.

With the increase in D.I.Y., manufacturers are slowly changing their view regarding spares supply. This is simply to fend off the patterned spares, by making the original parts more available and competitively priced. Again this will in turn benefit the consumer.

In conclusion

In the end, the decision between genuine and patterned spares is yours, but cost and speed of availability may have to be taken into consideration, but do not forsake quality for a small financial saving.

As a guide we have compiled a list of manufacturers' names and addresses where parts may be obtained. Addresses other than these can be found in your local Yellow Pages.

Parts by post

A free parts list of both patterned and genuine spares, catering for many of the above machines can be obtained from:-
Dixon Repair Services Ltd.,
(Postal Spares Department),
Hutton Cranswick,
Driffield,
North Humberside.
YO25 9QJ.

These parts can be obtained by post at very competitive prices and payment can be by cheque, Access or Visa.

Hoover	Has authorised dealer network locally. Spares available.
Hotpoint	Has authorised dealer network locally. Spares available.
Servis	Own network. Refer to the Yellow Pages. Spares available.
Indesit	Own network. Refer to the Yellow Pages. Spares available.
Zanussi	Authorised dealer network. Spares available.
Bendix	Own network. (Thorn-EMI). See Yellow Pages. Spares available. Bendix Customer Spares Dept., Angel Road, Edmonton, London. Tel 01-803-7383.
Candy	Has authorised dealer network locally. Spares available.
Electrolux	Own network. Refer to the Yellow Pages.
Philco	Has authorised dealer network locally. Spares available.
Fagor	Has authorised dealer network locally. Spares available.
Colston	See below.
Ariston	Spares available from Ariston Group Service. 0494-26420.
Philips	Spares available from Croydon. 01-686-0505.
Zerowatt	See Candy.
Creda	Distributor – Wharfdale Trading Co., Otley, 0943-465750.
Kelvinator	See Candy.

Chapter 27.

Know your machine

Know your machine

Most of us, you'll agree, would be completely lost without the range of gadgets we've become accustomed to using every day. Learning to take advantage of these time and energy-saving appliances, particularly in the kitchen, will give you the freedom to look after yourself and your family in more important ways.

With your special needs in mind, washing machine manufacturers have carefully developed automatic washing machines which will make the task quick and effortless however often you wash. There are several types of washing machines available.

Used properly, a fully automatic washing machine provides the most efficient and thorough method of washing. The special wash action of front and top loaders with a horizontal rotating drum mechanism creates sufficient agitation to effectively remove all dirt particles and even stubborn stains. However, it is important to use the correct type of washing powder in these machines. The low suds washing powder recommended by most major machine manufacturers is Persil Automatic. The free movement given by the controlled lather level lets the clothes be washed thoroughly and efficiently to give perfect results across all machine programmes, from a cotton boil wash to a cool programme for silk and woollens. Automatic machines will also ensure that sufficient rinses are made to remove the dirty wash solution leaving your clothes completely clean, fresh and cared for.

Overloading your machine will greatly reduce cleaning efficiency, as free movement of the clothes is restricted. Your machine has a maximum load capacity which should not be exceeded.

On the facing page is a handy table to help you check your dry weight loads compiled with the help of Lever Brothers.

Clothes

Blouse	cotton	150g	(5oz)
	other	100g	(3^1/$_2$oz)
Dress	cotton	500g	(1lb 2oz)
	other	350g	(12oz)
Dressing Gown		700g	(1lb 8oz)
Jeans		700g	(1lb 8oz)
10 Nappies		1000g	(2lb 3oz)
Nightdress		150g	(5oz)
Pyjamas	cotton	350g	(12oz)
Shirt	cotton	300g	(10oz)
	other	200g	(7oz)
Skirt		200g	(7oz)
Suit, bulked polyester		1500g	(3lb 5oz)
Sweater	wool	400g	(14oz)
	other heavy	350g	(12oz)
	lightweight	200g	(7oz)
Tracksuit		1000g	(2lb 3oz)
Teeshirt		125g	(4^1/$_2$oz)
Vest		125g	(4^1/$_2$oz)

Household items

Bedspread	candlewick	(D)	3000g	(6lb 10oz)
		(S)	2000g	(4lb 6oz)
Blanket	wool	(D)	2000g	(4lb 6oz)
		(S)	1500g	(3lb 5oz)
	acrylic	(D)	1500g	(3lb 5oz)
		(S)	1000g	(2lb 3oz)
Cot Sheet			200g	(7oz)
Duvet Cover	cotton	(D)	1500g	(3lb 5oz)
	other	(D)	1000g	(2lb 3oz)
Pillow			900g	(2lb)
Pillowslip			125g	(4^1/$_2$oz)
Tablecloth	large		700g	(1lb 8oz)
	small		250g	(9oz)
Tea Towels			100g	(3^1/$_2$oz)
Towel	bath		700g	(1lb 8oz)
	hand		250g	(9oz)
Sheet	cotton	(D)	1000g	(2lb 3oz)
		(S)	750g	(1lb 10oz)
	other	(D)	500g	(1lb 2oz)
		(S)	350g	(12oz)

Chapter 28.

Common causes of poor washing results

Common causes of poor washing results

Poor washing is mainly due to the wrong operation of the machine by the user, rather than a mechanical or electrical fault of the machine. The most common user faults are listed below.

1. Mis-use of the controls –

(a) To achieve good consistent results from your automatic, you must have a good understanding of your machine and its controls. Always remember – you tell the machine what to do. If in doubt, read the manufacturer's manual.
(b) Does the selected programme have the right water temperature and wash time for the fabrics in the load?

2. Incorrect dosage –

(a) The amount of powder that you should use is usually displayed on the side of the powder pack. Please remember that this is only a guide, and the amounts have to be adjusted to load size, type and degree of soiling, and the 'hardness' of the water supply.
(b) Is the container that is used for measurement of powder accurate? One measure of

powder should weigh 3oz.
(c) Have you made allowances for special types of soiling? Ointments, thick creams, heavy perspiration and the like, use up the suds activity very quickly. This can be compensated for by adding an extra half cupful of powder.

N.B. Poor soil and stain removal, the greying of whites or the appearance of 'greasy balls' on the washed clothes is a clear indication of under-dosing. It is never due to over-dosing.

3. Water supply –

Washing powder is formulated to do several tasks.
(a) Overcome water hardness.
(b) Wet-out the fabrics.
(c) Remove the soiling from the clothes.
(d) Hold the soiling in suspension, away from the clothes.

It can be seen that the harder the water, the harder the powder has to work. More powder should be added in the case of hard water, less in the case of soft water. The local area water authority should be able to

inform you of the hardness of water in your area.

4. Incorrect loading –

(a) Overloading the washer will result in the clothes not being able to move freely inside the drum, resulting in inadequate soil removal.
(b) Some programmes require reduced loads. If one of these programmes is used, reduce the load. If you are not sure, read the manufacturer's manual.

5. Other factors –

(a) How old is the machine? Like any purchase, a washing machine has a restricted lifespan. In the case of an automatic washer, the average lifespan is approximately eight years.
(b) When was the machine last serviced?
(c) Poor whiteness is a result of constant under-dosing (See 4). With the soiling not being removed, there is a gradual build up of deposits in the clothes. This can only be corrected by always washing with the correct loads.
(d) Domestic changes can reflect the quality of the wash, i.e., have

you moved area? (See 3.) Is there a new addition to the family? (see 2c.)

(e) Are the poor results evident on all programmes or only on specific programmes? (See 4.)

(f) Most of the manufacturers recommend an idle wash to keep the machine clean and free from deposits. This means a wash with no powder or clothes, every month or so.

(g) Have you read the manufacturer's manual?

Improvements on poor colours and whites will not happen magically, the process is very gradual. Once a good whiteness has been achieved, correct washing and dosing is the only way to maintain the standard.

Six golden rules for best results

1. Washing clothes frequently. Modern fabrics, particularly the man-made fibres, need frequent washing or dirt may become absorbed into the fibres.

2. Use the right amount of powder.
Refer to the side of the packet of powder for the correct dosage. Under dosing leads to poor soil and stain removal, and the greying of whites.

3. Choose the recommended wash code and machine programme for the fabric.
To safeguard colour and finish, preserve shape and minimise creasing, never wash hotter, wash longer or spin longer than indicated by the correct wash code for the fabric.

4. Rinse thoroughly.
Thorough rinsing is essential. Some finishes such as shower-proofing lose their effectiveness if not well rinsed; towelling fabrics, particularly nappies may become harsh and scratchy. Always rinse at least twice.

5. Treat stains quickly.
Give first aid treatment immediately wherever possible by blotting with an absorbent tissue. Never neglect a stain and never rub – this may push it further into the fabric. Pinch out as much as you can.

6. Dry 'easy care' fabrics correctly.
Check the instructions on the label. Easy care fabrics of cotton or man-made fibre, should be rinsed in cold water and should only be put in the spinner for a few seconds.

Chapter 29.

Successful stain removal

Successful stain removal

Stains on washable fabrics fall into two groups:

Group one – stains that will wash out in soap or detergent suds

Type of stain

Beetroot, Blood, Blackcurrant and other fruit juices, Chocolate, Cream, Cocoa, Coffee, Egg, Gravy, Ice lollies, Jam, Meat juice, Mud, Milk, Nappy stains, Pickles, Soft drinks, Sauces, Soup, Stews, Syrup, Tea, Tomato ketchup, Wines and Spirits and Washable ink.

Method

Fresh stains – Soak in cold suds to keep the stain from becoming set in the fabric. Then wash in the normal way according to the fabric.
Old dried-in stains – Lubricate with glycerine. Apply a mixture of one part glycerine to two parts water to the stain and leave for 10 minutes. Then treat as fresh stains.
Residual marks – White fabrics only. Bleach out with Hydrogen Peroxide solution. (One part 20 volume hydrogen peroxide to nine parts water). Leave soaking in this solution for 1 hour. Then wash in the normal way. Blood stains may leave residual iron mould marks, which should be treated as for iron mould.
Special Note: For 'built' stains such as egg (cooked), chocolate and mud, scrape off surplus staining matter first before putting to soak. Blood and meat juice stains whether fresh or old should be soaked in cold water first.

Group two – 'treat-'n-wash' stains

What you will need

Glycerine (for lubrication)
Methylated Spirit (handle carefully: *Inflammable – Poisonous).*
Turpentine *(Inflammable).*
Armyl Acetate (handle carefully – *Highly inflammable).*
Hydrogen peroxide.
Proprietary grease solvent – 'Thawpit', 'Beaucare', 'Dab-it-off', etc., *(Do not breathe the vapour: Use in a well ventilated room).*
Photographic Hypo.
White vinegar (acetic acid).
Household ammonia (keep away from eyes).
Cotton wool, Paper tissues, etc.

Handy hints

1. Act quickly to remove a stain and prevent it 'setting'. The faster you act, the milder the remedy needed.
2. Never rub a stain, as this pushes it further into the fabric. 'Pinch out' as much as you can, using a clean cloth or a paper tissue.
3. Never neglect a stain. The more drastic remedies for 'set' stains may harm delicate fabrics. If some stains are left on man-made and drip-dry fabrics in particular, they can be absorbed permanently into the fabric itself. Stains such as iron mould (rust) can weaken cellulosic fabrics and may eventually cause holes.
4. When applying solvents, always work from outside the stain towards the centre to avoid making a ring.
5. Always try a solvent on a hidden part first (e.g. under hem or seam allowance) to make sure it does not harm colours or fabric.
6. Stains on garments to be 'dry-cleaned' should be indicated

on the garment (e.g. with a coloured tacking thread). Tell the cleaners what has caused the stain. This facilitates the task of removal and lessens the risk of the stain becoming permanently set by incorrect treatment.

Absorbent pad method

Using two absorbent pads of cotton wool, one soaked with the solvent and other held against the stain. Dab the underside of the stain with solvent and the staining matter will be transferred from the material to the top pad. Change this pad around to a clean part and continue working in this way until no more staining matter comes through. To remove last traces of the stain, wash in usual way.

Type of stain	Solvent	Method
Ballpoint ink	Methylated spirit (INF) (Benzine for acetate and 'Tricel')	Absorbent pad method.
Bicycle oil	Proprietary grease solvent	Absorbent pad method or follow manufacturer's instructions
Black lead	Proprietary grease solvent	Absorbent pad method or follow manufacturer's instructions
Chalks and Crayons (Washable)		Brush off as much as possible while dry. Then brush stained area with suds (one dessertspoonful to a pint of water). Wash in the usual way.
Chalks and Crayons (Indelible)	Methylated spirit. (INF) (Benzine for acetate and 'Tricel'.) (INF)	Absorbent pad method
Chewing gum	Methylated spirit. (INF) (Benzine for acetate and 'Tricel'). (INF)	Absorbent pad method. Alternatively rub the gum with an ice cube to harden it. It may then be picked off by hand. Wash as usual to remove final traces.
Cod Liver Oil, Cooking Fat, Heavy grease stains	Proprietary grease solvent	Absorbent pad method or manufacturer's instructions
Contact adhesives. (e.g. Balsa cement, 'Evostick')	Amyl Acetate. (INF)	Absorbent pad method.
Felt pen inks	Methylated spirit. (INF) (Benzine for acetate and 'Tricel'). (INF)	First, lubricate the stain by rubbing with hard soap, and then wash in the usual way. for obstinate stains, use Methylated Spirit and absorbent pad method. Wash again to remove final traces.
Grass	Methylated spirit. (INF) (Benzine for acetate and 'Tricel'). (INF)	Absorbent pad method.
Greasepaint	Proprietary grease solvent	Absorbent pad method or follow manufacturer's instructions
Hair lacquer	Amyl Acetate, (INF)	Absorbent pad method
Iodine	Photographic Hypo	Dissolve one tablespoon hypo crystals in one pint warm water. Soak the stain for about 5 minutes, watching closely. As soon as the stain disappears, rinse thoroughly, then wash in the usual way.
Iron mould (rust marks)	a) Lemon juice (for wool, man-made fibres and all fine fabrics)	Apply lemon juice to the stain and leave it for 10-15 minutes. Place a damp cloth over the stain and iron. Repeat several times, as necessary. Rinse and wash as usual.
	b) Oxalic acid solution (for white cotton and linen only) use with care	Dissolve 1/2 teaspoonful oxalic acid crystals in 1/2 pint hot water. Tie a piece of cotton tightly round the stained area (to prevent the solution spreading) and immerse the stained part only. Leave for 2 or 3 minutes. Rinse thoroughly and wash in rich suds.

Washing Machine Manual

Type of stain	Solvent	Method
Lipstick and Rouge i) light stains ii) heavy stains	Proprietary grease solvent	Soak then wash in usual way. Absorbent pad method or follow manufacturer's instructions.
Marking ink	Marking ink eradicator (from stationers).	Follow instructions on the bottle label carefully.
Metal polish	Proprietary grease solvent	Absorbent pad method or follow manufacturer's instructions.
Mildew (mould on articles stored damp) a) coloured articles		The only treatment is regular soaking, followed by washing in rich suds – this will gradually reduce the marks.
b) white cottons and linens without special finishes.	Household bleach and vinegar.	Soak in one part bleach to 100 parts water with one tablespoonful vinegar. Rinse thoroughly, then wash.
c) white, drip-dry fabrics.	Hydrogen peroxide solution.	Soak in one part hydrogen peroxide (20 volume) and nine parts water until staining has cleared. Rinse thoroughly then wash in the usual way.
Nail varnish	Amyl Acetate for all fabrics (INF).	Absorbent pad method.
Nicotine (Tobacco juice).	Methylated spirit. (INF) (Benzine for acetate or 'Tricel'). (INF).	Absorbent pad method.
Non-washable ink	Oxalic acid solution. (For white cottons and linens only).	See method (b) under iron mould.
Paint: Emulsion	Water	Emulsion paint splashes sponged immediately with cold water will quickly be removed. Dried stains are pemanent.
Paint: Oil	Turpentine or Amyl Acetate. (INF).	Absorbent pad method.
Perspiration: Fresh stains	Ammonia. **Do not inhale the fumes.**	Damp with water, then hold over an open bottle of household ammonia.
Perspiration: Old stains	White vinegar	Sponge with white vinegar, rinse thoroughly, then wash in usual way.
'Plasticine' Modelling clay	Proprietary grease solvent or lighter fuel. (INF).	Scrape or brush off as much as possible. Apply solvent with absorbent pad method – wash to remove final traces.
Scorch: a) Light marks		Light stains will sometimes respond to treatment as for Group 1 – washable stains.
	Glycerine	If persistent, moisten with water and rub glycerine into the stained area. Wash through. Residual marks may respond to soaking in hydrogen peroxide solution.
b) Heavy marks	Heavy scorch marks that have damaged the fibres cannot be removed.	
Shoe polish	Glycerine and proprietary grease solvent	Lubricate stain with glycerine, then use solvent with absorbent pad method or follow manufacturer's instructions. Wash to remove final traces.

Type of stain	Solvent	Method
Sun tan oil	Proprietary grease solvent	Absorbent pad method or follow manufacturer's instructions.
Tar	Eucalyptus oil, Proprietary grease solvent, Benzine or lighter fuel. (NF).	Scrape off surplus, then apply solvent with absorbent pad method. Rinse and wash as soon as possible.
Verdigris (green stains from copper pipes, etc).		Treat as iron mould.

Special Note: Cotton garments with flame-resistant finishes must **not** be treated with household (chlorine) bleach or hydrogen peroxide in stain removal treatment, since this may impair the finish.

Keep solvents securely closed, labelled and out of children's reach.

Chapter 30.

Care labelling

Care labelling in the UK

To help housewives all over the country to know what washing conditions should be followed, the Home Laundering Consultative Council was formed from representatives of washing powder and washing machine manufacturers and the textile trade. The Council determined eight washing processes known as the British Textile Care Labelling Scheme and although this scheme has been superseded by a later more universal system, garment labels and washing machine controls and instructions produced under the eight British Codes will still be in evidence.

As from January 1974, a new system, the result of negotiations between the Home Laundering Consultative Council and the International Care Labelling Symposium, came into being. This is known as **The International Textile Care Labelling Code,** and the eleven wash codes determined under this system are reproduced in detail.

What the symbols mean

The wash tub symbol indicates a particular washing process most appropriate to a fabric or group of fabrics. It recommends:
The maximum safe washing temperature.
The amount of agitation during the wash.
The method of water extraction.

Agitation times

Maximum wash – means the longest agitation time for any machine as defined by the machine manufacturers.
Medium wash – is 40–60% of the maximum time.
Minimum wash – is 20–30% of the maximum time.
Hand wash – apply the label instructions as to the vigour of the wash to the particular circumstances. For fabric groups 6, 7 and 8 do not rub – squeeze the suds gently through the garment.

Water extraction

Instructions for this are in the main self-explanatory. It advises whether:
A cold rinse before spinning would be beneficial;
A long or short spin or no spinning or wringing is needed.
Note – Short Spin is the minimum spinning time as defined by the manufacturers for their appliance – e.g. 15 seconds only for man-made fibre fabrics, to avoid creasing.
When in doubt, spin-dry for the time necessary to remove surplus moisture only.

Other symbols within the International system

Bleaching

A triangle is the symbol used to indicate that bleach may be used.

Sometimes the triangle contains the letters 'Cl' which stands for chlorine. It therefore means a household (chlorine) bleach such as 'Domestos'.

If the symbol is crossed out, this means that household (chlorine)

bleach must **not** be used. If this instruction is ignored the fabric/finish/dye could be seriously affected.

Dry cleaning

 A circle is the symbol used for dry-cleaning instructions. It will never appear on its own but will have additional information as follows:

 Articles normal for dry-cleaning in all solvents.

 Articles normal for dry-cleaning in perchloro-ethylene, white spirit, Solvent 113 and Solvent 11.

 Articles normal for dry-cleaning in white spirit or Solvent 113.

 Do **not** dry-clean.

Ironing

 This symbol is used to provide ironing instructions. The number of dots within the symbol is varied to indicate the correct temperature setting, as follows:

 One dot = cool.

 Two dots = warm.

Three dots = hot.

 Crossed out = **do not iron.**

Drying

The vast majority of textile articles can safely be tumble dried. Care labels may be used to

indicate either that tumble drying is the optimum drying method for a particular article, or that tumble drying should not be used if the article is likely to be harmed by this treatment.

 Tumble drying beneficial.

Do **not** tumble dry.

In cases where the tumble drying prohibition symbol is used, any special positive instructions, such as 'dry flat' for heavier weight knitwear, should be given in words.

Explanation of drying symbols used by other countries

 Articles can be tumble-dried.

Drip drying is recommended.

Hang = line-dry.

Dry flat.

Mixed fabric group loads

Ideally fabric groups should not be mixed to make up a wash-load. Unless care is taken it does increase the risk of shrinkage, or dye contamination and discoloration of white things (particularly nylon) from articles which prove non-colourfast under the wash conditions. However, if for convenience or for the sake of economy, there is no alternative, always select the mildest wash conditions and use the following table as a guide:

Fabric codes 1 and 2 together – wash as code 2.
Fabric codes 3 and 4 together – wash as code 4.
Fabric codes 6 and 7 together – wash as code 6.
However, woollen garments must not be rubbed or hand wrung, as

this could distort the fibre. White nylon or articles from codes 5 and 8 should always be washed alone.

Fabric conditioning

No matter how thoroughly clothes are rinsed, after repeated washing and rinsing they gradually lose their bulk and softness. Fabric conditioner in the final rinse untangles matted fibres restoring the natural bulk and bounce to the fabric. But fabric conditioner is not only about softness on towels and woollens, it is about care for all your wash.

Special note on velvet

Velvet is a construction term, not a fibre. It may be silk, cotton or an acetate/nylon blend, e.g., 'Tricelon'. For best results look for the wash-care label and follow the instructions faithfully. If in doubt, dry-clean.

Soft furnishings in velvet weave, e.g., dralon – it is helpful to remove surface dust with a vacuum cleaner or soft brush. 'Dralon' velvet is not washable. It can be cleaned with a dry-foam shampoo. Avoid saturating cotton backing, vacuum or brush foam off when dry. When dry-cleaning, state fibre content.

Flame-retardant fabrics and finishes

Apart from nylon and wool, which are regarded as being of low flammability, there are two ways of giving fabrics flame-retardant properties:
(a) by the application to cotton fabrics of a special finish such as 'Proban', 'Pyrovatex', 'Timonox'. Also in certain cases to wool, though this as yet is not being widely used for apparel purposes.
(b) by the modification of the fibre itself, e.g., fibres like acrylic but with modified properties. The generic term for these is modacrylic, e.g., 'Teklan' or Monsanto's modacrylic. They are

inherently flame retardant.

The appropriate washing codes for the above are:

Code	Fabric
4/50	Cotton
7/40	Wool
6/40	Modacrylics

Important

Flame-retardant fabrics, e.g., modacrylics or fabrics with a flame-retardant finish must not be bleached, or soaked in any washing product.

Fabrics with a flame-retardant finish must not be washed in soap or non-automatic powder as soap can mask the properties of the finish. Other types of washing product, including automatic powder may be used with safety. Rinse very thoroughly.

Hand care

To get the best results in the hand wash make sure the powder is thoroughly dissolved before washing and the clothes thoroughly rinsed afterwards.

After each wash by hand, rinse your hands and dry them thoroughly. People with sensitive or damaged skin should pay particular attention to the instructions for use and avoid prolonged contact with the washing instructions.

If there is no wash care label on the garment, use the following A-Z to find the right fabric group code and full wash-care instructions.

'Special finish' labels

e.g. 'machine washable wool' — Sometimes the finish given to a fabric changes its washability. Where there is no wash-care guidance provided, check the name of the finish in the following A-Z to see whether there are any special care instructions.

No label provided

If you know what the fabric is, check the washing instructions in the A-Z. If in doubt wash under the mildest conditions, i.e., use warm 40°C suds only; do not soak; wash through quickly and gently; rinse thoroughly; blot off surplus moisture with a towel and dry carefully. If washing by machine choose the gentlest programme. If ironing seems appropriate, use a cool iron.

Labels with unfamiliar symbols

These will be found detailed.

Wash for the fabric, never mind the shape!

Remember always that it is the fabric and its construction rather than the type of article that decides the washing treatment. A polyester shirt will be grouped with a textured polyester suit, a small boy's polyester/'Viloft' trousers and his sister's polyester blouse. They are all different shapes and sizes but all will be washed as polyester requires, in hand-hot suds with cold rinsing and a short spin.

Different fabrics require different washing temperatures and agitation times. So ignore the *shape* of the article and concern yourself only with what it is made of and then wash it according to the appropriate Care Labelling Code and follow any special notes in the following A-Z.

Special guidance

Blends and mixtures

A *blend fabric* is one which has been woven or knitted from yarn made by the blending of two of more fibres, prior to the yarn being spun. A *mixture fabric* is one where two or more different yarns are used during weaving or knitting (e.g., a nylon warp woven into a viscose or cotton weft). In both cases the fibre which needs the milder treatment influences the wash conditions suitable for the fabric. For example a polyester/wool blend should only be washed in warm suds, because of the wool content; polyester/cotton and acrylic/cotton are both washed at temperatures lower than the maximum for cotton. If in doubt, wash as for the fibre requiring the milder treatment.

Colour fastness

Test for colour fastness by damping a piece of the hem or seam allowance and iron a piece of dry white fabric on to it. If any colour blots off, wash the article separately, in very cool suds, and rinse at once in cold water. Put to dry immediately. If the colour is very loose, dry cleaning may be advisable (check the label).

Soaking

There are occasions when heavily soiled or stained articles benefit from a soak before washing, particularly those included in fabric group code 1. Before soaking any coloured article it is important to make sure that:
The dye is fast to soaking – if in doubt do not soak;
The washing powder is completely dissolved before putting in the articles;
The water temperature is not too high for the fabric or the dye;
The article is not **bunched up** – it should be left as free as possible;
White and coloured articles are not soaked together – this is especially necessary where white nylon is concerned as nylon stockings and tights, for example, are seldom fast to soaking for long periods;
The articles do not have metal buttons or metal fasteners – soaking can encourage iron mould (brown stains).
Articles made from wool or silk or

from fabric with a flame-retardant
finish, whether white or coloured,
should *never be soaked in
washing products of any type.*

The International Textile Care Labelling Code

Symbol	Washing Temperature Machine	Hand	Agitation	Rinse	Spinning Wringing	Fabric	Benefits
1 / 95	very hot 95°C to boil	hand hot 50°C or boil	maximum	normal	normal	White cotton and linen articles without special finishes	Ensures whiteness and stain removal
2 / 60	hot 60°C	hand hot 50°C	maximum	normal	normal	Cotton, linen or viscose articles without special finishes where colours are fast at 60°C	Maintains colours
3 / 60	hot 60°C	hand hot 50°C	medium	cold	short spin or drip dry	White nylon, white polyester/cotton mixture	Prolongs whiteness- minimises creasing
4 / 50	hand hot 50°C	hand hot 50°C	medium	cold	short spin or drip dry	Coloured nylon; polyester; cotton and viscose articles with special finishes; acrylic/cotton mixtures; coloured polyester/cotton	Safeguards colour and finish – minimises creasing
5 / 40	warm 40°C	warm 40°C	maximum	normal	normal	Cotton, linen or viscose articles where colours are fast at 40°C but not at 60°C	Safeguards the colour fastness
6 / 40	warm 40°C	warm 40°C	minimum	cold	short spin	Acrylics; acetate and triacetate, including mixtures with wool; polyester/wool blends	Preserves colour and shape – minimises creasing
7 / 40	warm 40°C	warm 40°C	minimum do not rub	normal	normal spin do not hand wring	Wool, including blankets and wool mixtures with cotton or viscose silk	Keeps colour, size and handle
8 / 30	cool 30°C	cool 30°C	minimim	cold	short spin do not hand wring	Silk and printed acetate fabrics with colours not fast at 40°C	Prevents colour loss
9 / 95	very hot 95°C boil	hand hot 50°C or boil	medium	cold	drip dry	Cotton articles with special finishes capable of being boiled but requiring drip-drying	Prolongs whiteness, retains special crease-resistant finish

Do not machine wash

Do not wash

Expanded description of washing temperatures

100°C	Boil	Self-explanatory.	**50°C**	Hand-hot	As hot as the hands can bear.
95°C	Very hot	Water heated to near boiling temperature.	**40°C**	Warm	Pleasantly warm to the hand.
60°C	Hot	Hotter than the hand can bear. The temperature of water coming from many domestic hot taps.	**30°C**	Cool	Feels cool to the touch.

What it's called	What it is	Special notes	Wash code	Ironing notes
A				
Acetate	A cellulose derivative **fibre** fairly warm, soft, light, mothproof. Widely used in mixture fabrics.	Handle gently when wet. Take care with stain solvents.	[6/40] or [8/30]	Slightly and evenly damp on wrong side with **cool** iron.
'Acrilan'	See acrylics.		[6/40]	
Acrylics	Acrylic fibres have a warm soft handle yet are strong and hard-wearing. Good crease recovery. Do not shrink. Mothproof. Not affected by mildew.	Treat heavy knitted articles carefully when wet to avoid stretching.	[6/40]	**Cool** iron if required. To avoid stretching a knitted fabric it is often best to iron dry.
Actifresh	A bacteriostatic finish which prevents bacterial growth on synthetic fibres.		[6/40] or [4/50]	
Angora	Natural **fibre** obtained from the Angora rabbit. Warm, soft wool, with very fluffy surface.	Hand wash with care.	[hand wash]	Optional. **Warm** iron over **damp** cloth, or steam iron. Brush with teasel brush when **dry** to raise the surface.
B				
'Banlon'	A proprietary process for giving bulk, moderate stretch and extra warmth to synthetic thermoplastic yarns.		[3/60] White nylon [4/50] Others	**Warm** iron on **dry** fabric if necessary.
Bonded Fabrics	See laminates.			
Brushed Fabrics	Fabrics that have been brushed and the surface raised to provide extra warm handle e.g., brushed nylon, brushed viscose.	According to fabric. Check label.		Optional, **cool** iron when **dry**.
C				
Cashmere	Natural **fibre** consisting of downy undercoat of Tibetan cashmere goat. Very soft, warm handle; quickly felts with careless or over-vigorous washing.	Hand wash with care.	[hand wash]	Press on **wrong** side with **warm** iron under **damp** cloth to restore size, or use steam iron.
Cling Resist Nylon: 'Counterstat'	Nylon wth anti-static properties. Reduces 'cling' and 'riding up'. See nylon.			
Chloro fibres	See PVC			
'Clevyl T'	Trilobal chloro **fibre**.			
'Clydella'	A mixture **fabric** of natural fibres, wool and cotton woven together; lightweight, warm, ideal for baby wear.		[7/40]	Optional, **Warm** iron on **wrong** side when **damp**.
Corduroy	Cut-weft pile fabric with corded effect. Usually cotton.	Check label. Wash deep and bright colours separately. **Drip-dry.**	[4/50] [6/40]	**Do not iron.** If necessary remove creases by steaming.
Cotton	Natural **fibre**; strong, hard-wearing; stronger wet than dry, withstands vigorous washing processes without damage.		[1/95] W [2/60] C	**Hot** iron when **damp**.
'Courtelle'	See acrylics.			
'Crimplene'	See polyester. Textured 'Terylene' filament yarns which combine bulk with low stretch and offer excellent easy-care properties.	Used in men's wear and stretch covers.		

What it's called	What it is	Special notes	Wash code	Ironing notes
D				
Damask	An elaborately woven **fabric** used for furnishings, table linen, towels may be linen, cotton or viscose.	Creases easily, may be starched.		**Hot** iron on **right** side.
'Dacron'	See polyester.			
Denim	A construction term for a twill weave **fabric**, often cotton or cotton blends.	Not all denim is colourfast. Check label. Allow for shrinkage.	`1/95` W `2/60` `5/40` C	**Hot** iron when **damp**.
'Dicel'	See acetate.			
'Diolen'	See polyester.			
'Dralon'	See acrylics.	All Draylon fabrics are washable except woven velvet which must be dry-cleaned.		
Drip-dry cotton	Cotton which has been specially processed to give an easy-care, crease-resistant, minimum iron or non-iron finish.		`4/50`	Optional. **Warm** iron when **dry**.
'Durable Press'	See Permanent Press.			
'Dylan'	Proprietary process to impart shrink-resistance to wool. In some cases gives machine washability. Check with label.		`7/40`	Optional. **Warm** iron over a damp cloth; or use a steam iron.
'Dynel'	Modascrylic **fibre**. See flame retardant fibres.	Often used in fur fabrics.	`6/40`	
E				
Egyptian Cotton	Fine quality natural cotton **fibre**, made into closely woven cloth from Egypt; extremely hard wearing.		`1/95` W `2/60` C	**Hot** iron on **wrong** side when **damp**.
Elastane Fibres	Man-made stretch **fibres** with high rate of stretch recovery. Soft to the touch, light in weight. Used with other fibres for swimwear and foundation garments.	Wash according to other fabrics in weave, but **not** above 4. Check label.		**Do not iron.**
'Everglaze'	See glazed cotton.			
'Evalan'	Cellulosic, modified viscose **fibre**. Often blended with nylon, wool and acrylics.	Wash according to other fabrics in weave but **not** above 4. Evlan is most widely used in carpets but is used in some apparel.		
F				
'Fibreglass'	See Fibreglass.			
Fibreglass	**Fabric** woven from fine glass filaments. Resistant to bacteria, completely flame-proof. Drapes well. Does not sag or stretch.	Handle gently. Liable to fray if machine-washed. Abrasion can cause damage to the surface and loss of colour. **Drip dry**.	(hand wash)	**Do not iron.**
Fixaform'	See Permanent Press. A proprietary process which enables garments to retain pleats and shape.			

What it's called	What it is	Special notes	Wash code	Ironing notes
F (cond.)				
Flame Retardant Fabrics		Do not soak or bleach or boil.	[4/50] [6/40]	If necessary press **lightly on wrong** side whilst slightly damp. **Cool** iron.
Flame Retardant Finishes		Non-soap detergent wash only. Do not use soaps or soap products. Rinse carefully. **Never** soak or bleach.	[4/50]	**Cool** iron.
Flannelette	Flannel, a lightweight imitation of wool made from cotton or viscose mixtures.	Check label for colours. If made from any other fabric, wash according to fabric type. Check label.	[1/95] W [2/60] [5/40] C	**Hot** iron when slightly **damp**. As for fabric.
Foam Backs	**Fabrics** to which a layer of polyurethane or polyester foam has been bonded to the back of the face fabric to give warmth without weight and preserve shape.	Not all foam backs are suitable for home washing. If in doubt 'dry clean'. Washable foam backs should be laundered according to face fabrics. Always check label.		Iron according to face fabric.
G				
Glazed Cotton	Cotton with a special finish. Permanently glazed cotton will retain the high gloss; others lose their sheen on washing.		[4/50]	**Hot** iron on **wrong** side when **damp** Finish by polishing on **right** side.
Grosgrain Georgette Gaberdine	Names of particular types of weaves. May be silk, nylon, viscose, polyester, wool used in clothing fabrics.	Wash according to fibre type. Check label.		Iron according to fabric type.
H				
'Helenca'	A proprietary process used to impart high stretch to yarns such as nylon and polyester where a good stretch fit is desirable. Used for slacks and swimwear.		[3/60] White nylon [4/50] Others	**Warm** iron when **dry**, if necessary.
K				
Kenekalon 'Kopratron'	Modacrylic **fibre**. Trade name for 'Permanent or Durable Press' fabrics.		[4/50]	
L				
Lambswool	A natural **fibre**. Fine graded, high quality wool with exceptionally soft handle.	Hand wash with care.	[hand wash]	Press lightly with **warm** iron under **damp** cloth; or use steam iron. Brush up pile when dry.
Laminates	Two or more layers of fabrics bonded together to give strength, preserve shape, provide warmth without needing to line garment.	Not all laminates are suitable for home-washing. If in doubt 'dry-clean'. Washable laminates should be laundered according to face fabrics. Always check label.		Iron, if necessary, according to face fabric.
'Lastex'	A natural stretch yarn made from extruded rubber, used in corsetry, swimwear, ski wear.	Check garment label.		**Do not** iron.

What it's called	What it is	Special notes	Wash code Ironing notes	
Linen	Natural yarn **fibre** from flax. Very strong, washes and wears well.	Can be washed and ironed at high temperatures. Withstands bleaching and boiling if white.	[1 95 W] [2 60 C]	Hot iron when **damp**.
'Lirelle'	See polyester.			
'Lurex'	Proprietary name for specially processed metallic **threads** of various types to suit the yarn with which it is incorporated.	Wash as main fabric. Dry-clean where it is recommended.		**Warm** iron.
'Lycra'	See Elastane fibres.			
M				
'Marglass'	See Fibreglass.			
Minimum-iron	A finish obtained by special processing or weaving to impart easy-care properties and to eliminate ironing as far as possible.	According to fabric type. **Drip-dry**. Check label.	[3 60] [4 50] [6 40]	**Warm** iron when **dry** if necessary.
'Mitrelle'	Made from ICI **fibres**. Silk-like polyester yarns.			
Modacrylic	Class of man-made **fibre** contains 30–80% acrylonitrile, inherently flame retardant.	Check label.	[4 50]	**Cool** iron if necessary.
Modal	Viscose in modified form with improved wet strength, used mainly in blends with cotton or polyester.	Check label.	[2 60] [5 40]	Hot iron when **damp**. Warm iron if necessary for polyester blends.
Mohair	A natural **fibre** from the Angora goat. 'Long-haired' wool with exceptional warmth in wear.	Hand wash only.	[hand wash]	Press on **wrong** side under **damp** cloth with **warm** iron; or use steam iron. Brush up pile when dry.
Monsanto's Modacrylic	Modacrylic **fibre**. See flame-retardant fabrics. Used for pile fabrics, curtains, bedspreads.		[6 40]	
N				
Nylon	Strong, versatile synthetic **fibre**. Moth-proof; quick-drying, with good abrasion-resistance. Tends to build up static electricity and attracts dirt. Is 'low-flam'.		[3 60 W] [4 50 C]	**Warm** iron when **dry** if necessary.
P				
'Perlon'	See nylon.			
Permanent Press	A technique for giving permanent shape and creases to garments. Very suitable for men's trousers, rainwear, ski wear and stretch slacks.	According to fabric. **Do not wring.**	[4 50] [6 40]	Not necessary.
Polyester	Man-made fibre; very strong and hard wearing. Takes permanent pleats well, does not shrink or stretch. Mothproof. Mixes well with other fibres.	Attracts greasy soiling wash regularly.	[4 50]	**Warm** iron when **dry** if necessary.
Polyester/ Cotton	A blend of polyester and cotton yarns, giving the appearance and handle of cotton combined with the 'easy-care' and smooth drying of polyester.	Do not allow to become heavily soiled before washing.	[3 60 W] [4 50 C]	**Warm** iron when **dry** if necessary.

What it's called	What it is	Special notes	Wash code	Ironing notes
P (cond.)				
'Proban'	See flame-retardant finishes.	Non-soap detergent only. **Do not use soap.**	[4/50]	Cool iron.
P.V.C.	Polyvinyl chloride. A man-made thermo-plastic **fibre** which is chemically stable and non-flammable (i.e. does not burn without assistance). Water-repellent. Strong, wet or dry, but shrinks over 70°C. Softens at higher temperatures.	Soft fabrics. Used widely in upholstery and protective clothing. For coats and raincoats sponge only.	[6/40]	Do not iron.
'Pyrovaex'	See flame retardant finishes.	Non-soap detergent only. **Do not use soap.**	[4/50]	Cool iron.
Q				
'Quiana'	See nylon. 'Quiana' has a silk-like texture and soft handle.			
R				
'Rhonel'	See Triacetate.			
'Rhovyl'	See P.V.C.			
'Rigmel'	A proprietary finish used to impart shrink-resistance to cotton.		[6/40] [1/95]W [2/60]C	Hot iron when **damp**.
S				
'Sanforized'	Special finish giving shrink-resistance to cottons and fabrics likely to be washed regularly.	Wash as fabric type.		Iron as fabric type.
'Sarille'	Modified crimpled staple viscose. giving wool-like properties and drape. Used in dress-fabrics and blankets.		[5/40] damp.	Hot iron when slightly and evenly
'Scotchgard'	A water and oil repellent finish for clothing and furnishing fabrics, suitable for home washing or dry-cleaning.	Wash as fabric. Rinse very thoroughly. **Drip-dry.**		**Warm** iron if necessary.
Shantung	Wild silk with a slub incorporated in the weave – see silk.			
Silk and Wild silk	Natural protein **fibre** from the silkworm. Very soft handle with luxurious appearance. Creases easily but creases fall out. Expensive. Used in luxury fabrics.	Rinse thoroughly. Dry gently.	[7/40] [8/30]	**Warm** iron when slightly and evenly **damp**; wild silk **cool** iron when **dry**.
'Spanzelle'	See Elastane fibres. Spanzelle has been withdrawn. May still be found in textiles for some time.			
'Superwash' Wool	Now known as 'Machine Washable Wool'. A polymer process giving shrink-resistance to wool. In most cases also imparts machine washability whilst retaining softness. Check with label.		[7/40]	**Warm** iron over a **damp** cloth or use steam iron.
T				
'Teklan'	See flame-retardant fabrics. A Modacrylic fibre.		[6/40]	
'Tendrelle'	See Nylon.			

What it's called	What it is	Special notes	Wash code	Ironing notes
'Tergal'	See Polyester.			
'Terital'	See Polyester.			
'Teryline'	See Polyester.			
'Tetron'	See Polyester.			
'Timonox'	See Flame Retardant Finishes.	Synthetic detergent only. **Do not use soap.**	4/50	**Cool** iron.
'Trevira'	see Polyester.			
'Triacetate'	Man-made cellulosic derivative **fibre**, easy to match, does not shrink or stretch. More robust in wash and wear than acetate. Good drape, silky handle.	For pleated garment – check label.	6/40	**Cool** iron when **damp.**
'Tricel'	See Triacetate.			
Trilobal	Technical term to describe fibres with a rounded triangular cross-section which gives improved handle and appearance.			
Tussore	Wild silk incorporating a slub in the weave – see silk.			
U				
'Ultron'	Nylon with anti-static properties. Reduces 'cling' and 'riding-up.' See nylon.			
V				
Velvet	See Special Notes.			
'Verel'	Modacrylic staple **fibre** for pile fabrics and carpets.			
'Viloft'	A tubular viscose **fibre** with high bulk and extra absorbency usually mixed with polyester or acrylic.	Washes well often used in leisure garments because of comfort characteristics. Used extensively in sportswear, underwear, including thermal.	4/50	
Viscose	Widely used man-made cellulosic **fibre** used on its own, as a mixture fabric or blended with other yarns. Pleasant handle and drapes well; good dyeing properties. (Formerly rayon or viscose rayon).		2/60	**Hot** iron on **wrong** side when **damp.**
'Viyella'	Mixture **fabric** of 55% lamb's wool and 45% cotton with a warm, soft handle, suitable for babies' and children's wear. More recently developed for top fashion clothes.		7/40	**Warm** iron on **wrong** side whilst slightly **damp.**
W				
Water	**Fabrics** given special finish to confer some resistance to water penetration.	Avoid detergents. Wash according to fabric type in soap powder. Rinse very thoroughly. **Dry-dry.** Check label.		**Warm** iron if necessary.
Wool	Natural **fibre** from the sheep; available in several qualities. Warm, soft handle.	Hand wash unless article carries machine label.	7/40	**Warm** iron under **damp** cloth or steam iron.

Chapter 31.

Jargon

Jargon

Armature – Wire wound centre of brush motor.
Bi-metal – Two different metals, that have been joined together. When heated the strip bends in a known direction.
Burn-out – Overheated part or item.
Carbon face (seal) – Watertright flat surface seal.
Clamp band – Large adjustable clip used for holding door boot.
Closed circuit – A normal circuit that allows power to pass through.
Commutator – Copper segment on motor armature.
Contact – Point at which switch makes contact.
Continuity – Electrical path with no break.
Component – Individual parts of the machine, i.e., pump, valves, motor, are all components.
Corbin – Type of spring hose clip.
Dispenser – Compartment that takes washing powder.
Dispenser Hose – Hose that supplies the tub with detergent and water from the dispenser compartment.
Drift – Soft metal rod used for bearing removal.
Door Boot – Flexible seal between door and tub.
Early – Machine not currently on market.
Energize (Energise) – To supply power to.
Energized (Energised) – Having power supplied to.
E.L.C.B. – Earth leakage circuit breaker – see R.C.C.B.
Flowchart – Method of following complicated steps in a logical fashion.
Functional test – To test machine on a set programme.
Garter ring – Large elasticated band used to secure door boot.
Grommet fitting – Method of fitting hoses, etc., whilst requiring no clips.
Harness – Electrical wiring within a machine.
Impeller – The blades of the pump that pump the water.
Isolate – To disconnect from the electricity supply and water supply, etc.
Laminations – Joined metal parts of parts of stator.
Lint – Fluff from clothing that may cause a small blockage.
Late – Current machine on market.

Make – 1. Manufacturer's name.

          2. When a switch makes contact, it is said to 'make'.

Open-circuit – Circuit that is broken, i.e., will not let any power through.

Porous – Item that allows water to pass through.

Programmer – See Timer.

P.S.I. – Measurement of water pressure, pounds per square inch, i.e., 38 p.s.i.

R.C.C.B. – Residual current circuit breaker (also known as R.C.D.)

Rotor – Central part of an induction motor.

Schematic Diagram – Theoretical diagram.

Seal – Piece of pre-shaped rubber that usually fits into a purpose built groove, therefore creating a watertight seal.

Sealant – Rubber substance used for ensuring watertight joints.

Shell – Outer of machine.

Spades – Connections on wires or components that are pulled off gently.

Stat – Thermostat.

Stator – Electrical winding on motor.

Syphon – A way of emptying the machine via gravity.

Terminal block – A method of connecting wires together safely.

Timer – Programme switch.

T.O.C. – Thermal Overload Cut-Out. At a pre-set temperature, the T.O.C. will break electrical circuit to whatever it is attached, i.e., prevents motors, etc., overheating.

Changes in wash coding – October 1987 onwards

From October 1987 a change in the clothes labelling is due to be introduced. We show here a comparison chart between old and new styles. This should help in the transition period when you will have garments bearing both types of labelling. The idea is to give more information on the garment itself, to aid washing and whether or not to mix loads etc. In the long run, such information will be most helpful and we believe welcomed by all.

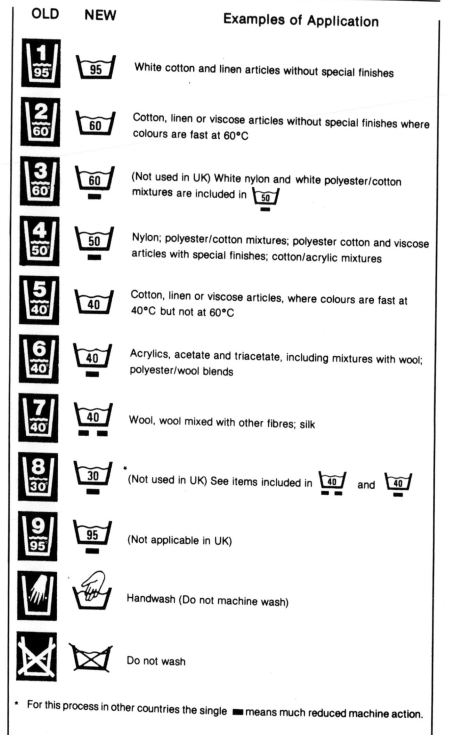

OLD	NEW	Examples of Application
1 / 95°	95	White cotton and linen articles without special finishes
2 / 60°	60	Cotton, linen or viscose articles without special finishes where colours are fast at 60°C
3 / 60°	60	(Not used in UK) White nylon and white polyester/cotton mixtures are included in [50]
4 / 50°	50	Nylon; polyester/cotton mixtures; polyester cotton and viscose articles with special finishes; cotton/acrylic mixtures
5 / 40°	40	Cotton, linen or viscose articles, where colours are fast at 40°C but not at 60°C
6 / 40°	40	Acrylics, acetate and triacetate, including mixtures with wool; polyester/wool blends
7 / 40°	40	Wool, wool mixed with other fibres; silk
8 / 30°	30	*(Not used in UK) See items included in [40] and [40]
9 / 95°	95	(Not applicable in UK)
(handwash)	(handwash)	Handwash (Do not machine wash)
(do not wash)	(do not wash)	Do not wash

* For this process in other countries the single ■ means much reduced machine action.

MIXING WASH LOADS

As a general guide you can mix wash labels without a bar provided you wash at the lowest temperature shown.

e.g. ⌴60⌴ and ⌴40⌴ can be washed together at 40°C.

Likewise, you can mix wash labels with and without a bar provided that, again, you wash at the lowest temperature, BUT you must also reduce the washing action.

e.g. ⌴60⌴ and ⌴40⌴ can be washed together at 40°C at a reduced action.

Articles with ⌴40⌴ must be washed as wool at a much reduced action.

REMEMBER "wash separately" means what it says.

EXAMPLES OF THE NEW LABEL FORMATS

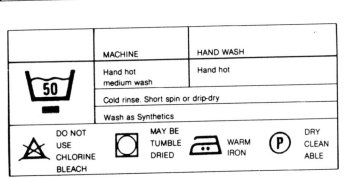

3112